THE GREY EAGLES

of

CHIPPEWA FALLS

THE GREY EAGLES
of
CHIPPEWA FALLS

A Hidden History of a Women's Ku Klux Klan in Wisconsin

JOHN E. KINVILLE

Published by The History Press
Charleston, SC
www.historypress.com

Front cover: Grey Eagles near Chippewa Falls, circa 1927. *Author's collection.*
Back cover: The WKKK distributed stickers promoting public schools in response to the presence of Catholic parochial schools, circa 1924. *Author's collection.*

First published 2020

Manufactured in the United States

ISBN 9781467144810

Library of Congress Control Number: 2019951877

To Mom and Dad, for instilling empathy and tolerance.

CONTENTS

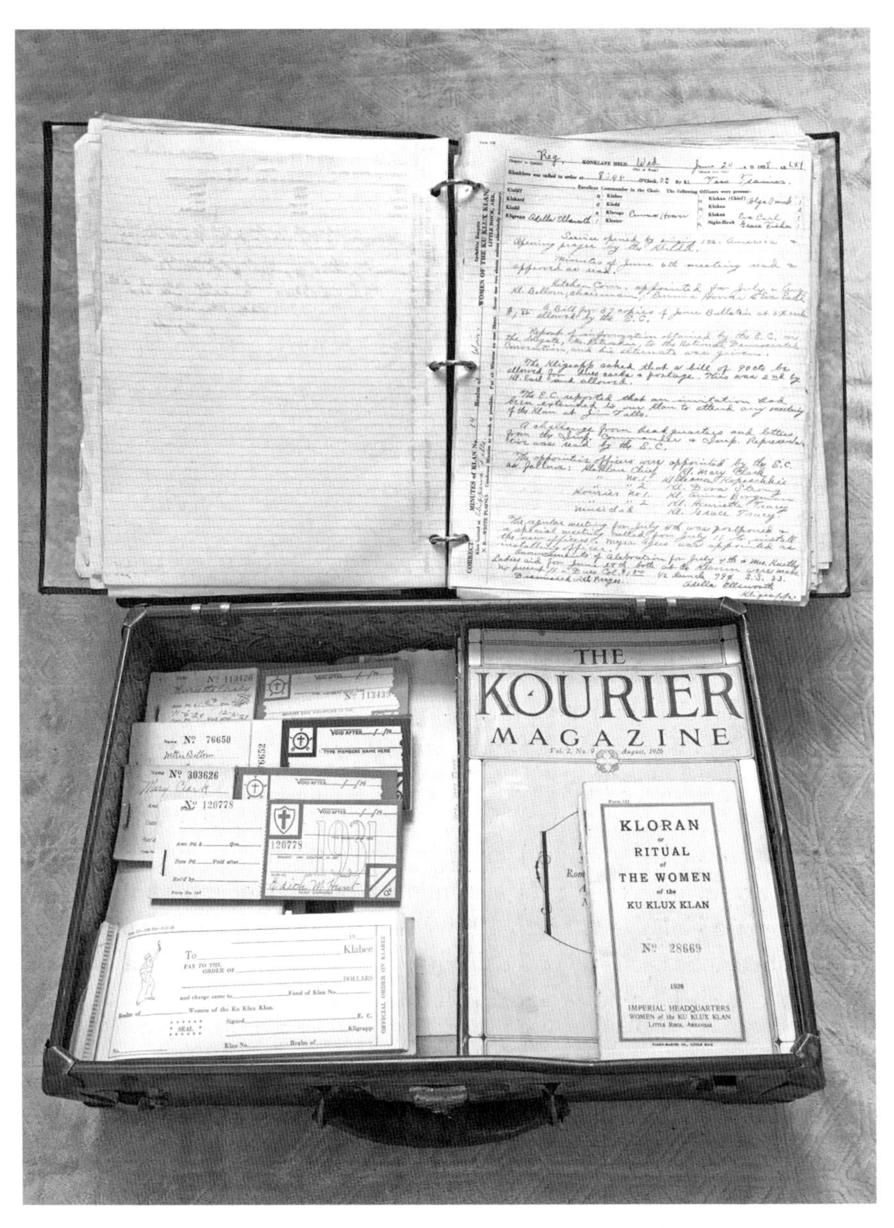

Original records from the Chippewa Falls unit of the WKKK, including meeting minutes, financial records and other ephemera. *Private collection.*

PREFACE

My journey to develop *The Grey Eagles of Chippewa Falls* began as a young man in the Lake Hallie and Chippewa Falls region of western Wisconsin. I routinely heard stories about the Ku Klux Klan in the area, including clandestine meetings, elaborate ceremonies, picnics and chicken dinners and crosses burning atop the few nearby hills. Aside from scattered oral accounts, little tangible evidence remained from their presence in the 1920s and '30s.

While studying as an undergraduate at the University of Wisconsin–Eau Claire, I came across a set of documents within the university's archive that changed my life forever. The file was named "Women of the Ku Klux Klan 14 (Chippewa Falls, Wis.), 1926-1931." As I thumbed through each page, I was stunned. The cache recorded the activities of the women of the Ku Klux Klan unit from Chippewa Falls. It included the biweekly inner workings of an organization known for its intense secrecy. Included were financial records, regional bulletins, national correspondences, official publications, a membership list, miscellaneous ephemera and a written set of minutes from fifty-eight meetings. Nearly sixteen years later, I have finally put my interest in this topic into writing.

ACKNOWLEDGEMENTS

This book would not have been possible without the support of the Wisconsin State Historical Society, Chippewa County Historical Society, Chippewa Valley Museum, Dunn County Historical Society and the University of Wisconsin–Eau Claire's special collections department.

Special thanks to John Rodrigue at The History Press, John and Carolyn Kinville, Mike and Tristi Crawford, Kim and Mary Jane Henderson, Chris and Shannon Elwell, Orrin and Naomi Todahl, David and Sandra Martineau, Mark and Lori Isaacson, Dylan Helwig, Tamara Harris, Alondra Harris, Zach Elbert, Brian Curran, Tucker Melssen, Angela Gudmanson, Scott and Tammy Tillotson, Patrick and Toma Kinville, Jim and Claudia Kinville, David and Barbara Kinville, Joe and Carolyn Kinville, Will and Abbie Steiger, Michael Kramer, Matt and Leya Hoy, Anya Schreiner, David H. Raihle Jr., Connie Zook, Sheila Hansen, Kris Taylor, Judy Baier, Winifred Jensen, Amanda Hill-Hable, Jeff at atlantarelics.com and the many grandchildren of the Grey Eagles who helped me get this book across the finish line.

I want to recognize the teachers, professors and support staff of the Chippewa Falls School District, University of Wisconsin–Eau Claire and the University of Wisconsin–River Falls. Without your dedication and love for learning, I would not be the person I am today, especially John P. Kaminski, Oscar Chamberlain, Susan Krueger, Kurt Leichtle, James

Oberly, Jane Pederson, Roger Tlusty, Robert Gough, Selika Ducksworth-Lawton, Tom Frederick, Roger Thompson and Darrin Ekern.

Lastly, none of this would be possible without the loving support and patience of my family, including my children, Jack, Jonathan and Savannah, as well as my cats, Huey, Ghost and Lizzie. My wife, Kara, deserves the biggest thanks of all, as she never once doubted my abilities in completing this book. She was a steady supporting partner throughout all phases of the project.

INTRODUCTION

While much is known about the men's Ku Klux Klan of the 1920s and '30s, the same cannot be said for its female membership. Due to the absence of detailed or comprehensive historical evidence to work from, little is known about the day-to-day inner workings of the female Klavern. As a result, much of the historiography has centered on the activities of the men. In 1987, Professor David Chalmers, nationally renowned author of *Hooded Americanism: The History of the Ku Klux Klan*, wrote the most comprehensive history of the men's Klan. Chalmer's fifty-state focus covered the Klan's post–Civil War origins, its rebirth and meteoric rise in the 1920s and, finally, the post–World War II fight against racial integration. Unfortunately, Chalmers' coverage of the Women's Ku Klux Klan was limited to brief appearances within the sprawling volume.[1]

In 1991, Professor Kathleen Blee published *Women of the Klan: Racism and Gender in the 1920s*. Considered the most exhaustive book on women of the Ku Klux Klan to date, Blee meticulously revealed how the women's order was not incidental to, nor subservient to, the directives of the men's Klan. Instead, Blee unveiled a complex organization of like-minded, patriotic women who fought passionately for social improvement through charity work and social causes like temperance, women's suffrage, public education and strong religious observance as being vital to a stable home and society.[2]

Paradoxically, this nativist yearning for an improved "100 percent American" society, which was rooted in their supposed adoration of freedom and the U.S. Constitution, took the form of a malicious ideology featuring a potent mixture of anti-Semitism, racism and xenophobia. Similar to their male counterparts, the members of the WKKK were fearful and antagonistic toward nonwhites, non-Protestant Christians and violators of the nation's anti-alcohol Prohibition laws. Across the nation, the primary targets of the WKKK were African Americans, Catholics, Jews, socialists, immigrants, labor unions, bootleggers and any "other" person who was deemed unworthy of the label "100 percent American."[3]

While sensational headlines of horrific and brutal acts of the male Klan appear ad nauseam throughout the 1920s and '30s, the WKKK received little negative national or regional headlines from the "white press." In her book, Blee uncovered a women's organization filled with a more nuanced experience than its male counterpart. For all intents and purposes, the female members of the Klan were more charitable, law-abiding and committed to reflecting the positive ideals preached by both the KKK and the WKKK.[4]

Even their anti-Semitic, racist and xenophobic views materialized differently than those of the men. Rather than overt physical violence, which were salaciously covered in the press and destructive to the reputation of Klan men, the weapon of choice for female members were covert "poison squads." Whether these squads were purposely planned to wreak havoc on opponents or merely formed as the natural byproduct of verbal gossip and whispering rumors, innuendo and slander could be venomously passed through a community, leading to mistrust, destroyed reputations, economic boycotts or a whole litany of misfortunes for the recipients.[5]

More recently, however, there is a growing body of research that suggests the Women of the Ku Klux Klan in the 1920s and '30s, was more "mainstream" and "normal" than past historians admit. In *Everyday Klansfolk: White Protestant Life and the KKK in 1920s Michigan*, independent scholar Craig Fox finds similar evidence. Sifting through recently discovered Klan documents pertaining to a men's chapter in Newaygo County, Fox uncovered a 1920s Klan that provided a social activist outlet that transcended socioeconomic, gender and age divisions. For a brief window, the Klan was viewed as one of the most respected, family-orientated, patriotic and religiously minded organizations that Protestant whites could belong to.[6] As Blee was surprised to learn in interviews with former Klanswomen in Indiana, former members viewed their time in the organization with fondness and nostalgia, not with shame or regret.[7]

In the 1920s and '30s, the national WKKK became a major vehicle for conservative women to earn social advancement within the white Protestant world's tightly controlled gender roles. Often through self-desire or external encouragement from their husbands, an estimated five hundred thousand women became members of the WKKK. This intensely secret organization provided members with ample opportunities to achieve social, political and civic change within their communities. Each locally chartered Klavern, or chapter, was expected to carry out its own meetings and rituals, tend to its own financial needs and challenges and politically mobilize around key issues of the day. Hundreds of Klaverns throughout the nation were composed strictly of women and were operated almost solely by women. Attending a Klavern gave members an empowering feeling that was enjoyed with other like-minded women and was mostly experienced away from the close monitoring of their husbands.

In June 2017, on the website Timeline, which specializes in news stories and editorials featuring women's history, managing editor Laura Smith posted an article titled "The KKK Started a Branch for Women in the 1920s, and half a million joined: The platform mingled racism, nativism, and...feminism?" Smith implied that the women's auxiliary of the Klan helped usher in a historically bizarre brand of feminism that quietly and carefully changed the female gender roles within the extreme conservative wing of Protestant society. Through charities, picnics, parades, fundraising socials and the hosting of political speakers, the 1920s WKKK were subtlty empowering themselves in a patriarchal world where women in positions of power were often viewed poorly.[8]

Unfortunately, these modest gains in social standing and political power came at the expense of millions of other American citizens, with whom the women of the Klan helped to target, marginalize and, ultimately, undermine. Blee also seemed to struggle with the final resting place of the WKKK in American social history, writing, "Klanswomen held reactionary political views on race, nationality, and religion. But their views on gender roles were neither uniformly reactionary nor progressive."[9] Is it possible, then, that the Women of the Ku Klux Klan did indeed usher in a historically anomalous strain of feminism that originated in the extreme right-wing of the American political and cultural spectrum?

This book seeks to answer these questions through the careful analysis of the meeting minutes taken by a WKKK chapter in Chippewa Falls, Wisconsin. Calling themselves the Grey Eagles, the female membership of WKKK Klan no. 14 held fifty-eight official meetings from 1927 through 1931. These minutes provide revealing answers to some of history's most enduring questions regarding the female membership within the hooded order: Who were these women? Were they marginal figures in their communities? What took place inside a Klavern? What topics and issues did they discuss? What causes did they champion? Did they leave written evidence of their animosities? Was violence ever planned or discussed? And, finally, did they achieve any social advancements within the white Protestant community in western Wisconsin?

PART I

THE BIRTH, RISE, FALL AND REBIRTH OF THE KU KLUX KLAN

I

GHOULS IN THE NIGHT

Southern Origins and Post–Civil War Terrorism

The creation of the Ku Klux Klan took place in 1865, shortly after the end of the Civil War, in the small, southern city of Pulaski, Tennessee. The all-male organization seemed harmless enough, as the founding members came from the middle and upper strata of southern society, including college-educated men and military officers. As Klan historian David Chalmers wrote, "Their problem was idleness. Their purpose was amusement."[1]

Inspired by the Greek word *kuklos*, meaning "ring" or "circle," and the Gaelic word *clan*, meaning "children" or "progeny," members of the Ku Klux Klan attended secluded meetings, held secret initiations, wore concealing costumes and engaged in late-night "horseplay." This intoxicating mixture of excitement and mysticism fueled the Klan's popularity and led to the group's quick expansion into neighboring locales. Similar to the problems associated with the South's confederal model of government during the Civil War, the Pulaski Klan was unable to control the actions and behavior of its ever-multiplying satellite units.[2]

Individual Klans quickly evolved into reactionary paramilitary and vigilante groups. They sought to reverse the political, social and economic changes wrought by the Thirteenth, Fourteenth and Fifteenth Amendments to the U.S. Constitution. Newly empowered African Americans throughout the South were improving their lives under the protection of federal troops during Reconstruction. These newly enfranchised voters quickly changed the political and racial make-up of their state legislatures, thus empowering them to confront the laws that served as the foundation of the southern white male power structure.

Towering above all other fears that southern white men held against newly empowered black men was the fear of losing their racial purity. The symbolism that these men attributed to southern white women was culturally rooted within the "core of his sense of property and chivalry." Because white women had been made culturally and historically inaccessible to black men, they represented the "ultimate line of difference between white and black" in the South. While the North viewed Reconstruction as a period of physical rebuilding the southern economy, southern white men viewed it as further deterioration of their way of life.[3]

Seen as an effective means of restoring the white hierarchy, KKK units were vehicles to engage in acts of intimidation, vandalism, assault and murder. Violent night raids carried out by imposing and ghostly posses of costumed riders on horseback wreaked havoc throughout the South. Citing his own personal concerns over the Klan's escalating association with violence, the group's leader, Grand Wizard and former confederate lieutenant General Nathan Bedford Forrest, ordered the fractious organization to be dissolved. Forrest's decree fell mostly on deaf ears as individual Klans became increasingly independent. Klan vigilantism remained rampant.[4]

By 1871, after reports of continued Klan mayhem, President Ulysses S. Grant prompted Congress to pass the Ku Klux Klan Act. The legislation allowed the national government to suspend a suspected Klansman's writ of habeas corpus, which enabled the federal military to arrest, fine and imprison those directly associated with a terrorist organization. The enforcement led to a precipitous decline in Klan activity, as well as the group's purported demise in 1872. Just five years later, the end of Reconstruction and the removal of federal troops from the South enabled southern white Democrats to quickly recapture their respective statehouses. Nearly all of the political, economic and social gains made by African Americans throughout the South had been reversed.[5] Meanwhile, the Ku Klux Klan disappeared.

2

THE BIRTH OF A NATION

The Klan Resurrected in Film

The revival of the Ku Klux Klan began in 1915 with the help of Hollywood. Based on the 1905 novel *The Clansman* by Thomas Dixon Jr., filmmaker D.W. Griffith's *The Birth of a Nation* became one of the most popular and controversial movies of the early 1900s. The groundbreaking silent film featured a love story set during the Civil War and Reconstruction. The nearly three-hour production was heralded by members of the national press for its authentic portrayal of Abraham Lincoln's assassination, as well as the scale and scope of battle scenes. Newspaper advertisements billed the movie as "The World's Mightiest Spectacle" and Griffith's "8th Wonder of the World." After President Woodrow Wilson enjoyed a personal screening at the White House, he added to the film's credibility by claiming, "It is like writing history with lightning…and my only regret is that it is all so terribly true."[6]

Although Griffith rightfully earned acclaim for showing "war as it actually is," his portrayals of African Americans and the Ku Klux Klan were disturbingly inaccurate. Played by white actors in blackface, African Americans were depicted as "uncouth, intellectually inferior, and predators of white women."[7] The movie concluded with a wildly heroic Ku Klux Klan horse-riding scene featuring the film's protagonist—a dashingly handsome white southern male—rescuing an endangered white southern belle from the hands of a sexually deranged black brute. Despite organized protests from groups like the National Association for the Advancement of Colored People (NAACP), the film achieved towering financial success at the box office.[8]

Advertisement from the 1930 rerelease of *The Birth of a Nation. Author's collection.*

Residents of Chippewa Falls, Wisconsin, had their first opportunity to view the film during the week of Thanksgiving at the Unique Theatre in nearby Eau Claire. Touted as the "Most Tremendous Dramatic Spectacle the Brain of Man has Yet Produced," a half-page advertisement in the *Chippewa Herald* argued that seeing the film "Will Make a Better American of You." As western Wisconsin attendees sold out showings for the entire week, D.W. Griffith's inaccurate portrayal of the Klan was engrained in unsuspecting moviegoers' minds across the country. The Klan was no longer a forgotten terrorist organization but a heroic and inspirational force that protected women through the application of law and order.[9]

One man captivated by the onscreen heroics of the fictional Klan was a former southern preacher named William J. Simmons. While recuperating from an automobile accident, Simmons hatched a plan to revive the Klan as a fraternal social order. On the evening of Thanksgiving, November 25, 1915, Simmons and a group of fifteen men climbed Stone Mountain outside of Atlanta, Georgia, and burned a fiery cross for all in the area to see. In an article titled "Klan Is Established with Impressiveness," the *Atlanta Constitution* reported that the Knights of the Ku Klux Klan were formed by Simmons to take an "active part in the betterment of mankind" and would organize under the Latin motto *Silba*

The USS *Hawk* was the birthplace of the Klan in Wisconsin. *Author's collection.*

Sed Anthar ("Not for one's self but for others").[10] Moviegoers enthralled by the mysticism and heroics of the silver screen Klan would soon have the opportunity to join a living manifestation.

In 1920, roughly five years after Simmons's revival in Atlanta, the first Wisconsin men's Klan unit was organized in Milwaukee. A small group of prominent men from the city's professional and business classes boarded the USS *Hawk*, a former private yacht that had been modified into a naval training vessel and was moored in the Milwaukee River.[11] There they formed Wisconsin Klan no. 1, otherwise known as the Milwaukee Businessman's Club.[12] Although it would take nearly six years for the Klan to spread across the rest of Wisconsin, an internal bulletin from 1926 revealed that fifty-seven men's Klans had been chartered in Wisconsin, leaving few sections of the state untouched by its presence.[13]

3

AGITATED BADGERS

Race, Liquor, Catholicism and "100 Percent Americanism"

In addition to being part of a heroic organization witnessed on the big screen, an individual's rationale for joining the Klan was more complicated than one might assume. In a pamphlet titled "Ideals of the Women of the Ku Klux Klan," the organization professed their allegiances to "God and Government, Law and Liberty, Peace and Prosperity, and America for Americans." Civically, they promoted voting, a free press, a clean government, respect for the American flag and a strong adherence to the principles of the Declaration of Independence and the U.S. Constitution. Socially, the hooded order advocated for strong public schools, faithful religious observance and traditional family values, including abstention from alcohol, gambling, prostitution, dance halls and other vices. According to the example set forth within Klan literature, members were expected to be model citizens acting directly on behalf of their Protestant Christian God. This celebration of all things patriotic became known as "100 percent Americanism."[14]

What set the Klan apart from most other social clubs of the era was the group's extensive target list, which included criminals, bootleggers, organized crime figures, unions, communists, socialists, migrants, immigrants and a wide array of religious, racial and ethnic minority groups. Many joined the Klan because of its emphasis on the "eternal supremacy of the white race," manifested in a goal of keeping whites and minorities from engaging in sexual intercourse or producing biracial children. The

Remember
EVERY
Criminal
Thug
Gambler
Libertine
Girl Ruiner
Home Wrecker
Wife Beater
Dope Peddler
Moonshiner
Crooked Politician
Pagan Catholic Priest
Shyster Lawyer
K. C.
White Slaver
Brothel Madam
Rome Controlled
Newspaper
Black Spider
Is Fighting the Klan
THINK IT OVER.
WHICH SIDE ARE YOU ON?

Above: The WKKK distributed stickers promoting public schools in response to the presence of Catholic parochial schools, circa 1924. *Author's collection.*

Left: Propaganda card designed to increase membership, circa 1924. *Author's collection.*

Klan focused on the "protection of pure American womanhood" from a biological and cultural standpoint, based on eugenics.[15] Popular during the early twentieth century, eugenics is the science that the human species can be improved through selective mating with those who possess desirable heredity traits. Supporters, including the Klan, believed that most problems could be "bred out" of the human species, including "disease, mental illness, criminal tendencies, and even poverty."[16] Skin color variations were seen as a major flaw within the human race.

Most Klan literature from the era proclaimed that the "negro should be protected in every way possible," and Klansmen should "readily fight for their constitutional rights" as if they were their own. The Klan argued, "We would not rob the colored population of their rights, but we demand that they respect the rights of the White Race in whose country they are permitted to reside." For the typical Wisconsin Klansmen in the 1920s, they would not condone physical harm to anyone, black or white. In fact, many prided themselves on being descendants of Civil War veterans who had been instrumental in ending slavery in the United States.[17]

In the South, by contrast, many Klansmen viewed the literature on race as a form of coded permission to engage in violence and acts of terrorism against African Americans. It was rumored that Imperial Wizard Dr. Hiram Evans had personally directed and participated in violence against blacks while in the South.[18] With the exception of Wisconsin's southeastern urban centers, including Beloit, Kenosha, Racine and Milwaukee, the 1920 population of African Americans was sparse. In Chippewa County, for example, there were just twenty-four African Americans in a population of thirty-six thousand.[19] For Chippewa Falls residents, there were other perceived threats that brought them into the fold.

Much of the popularity of the KKK in Chippewa County derived from a complex amalgamation of fears and concerns regarding alcohol, Catholicism and immigration. While each would have been viewed as a separate target list by the national headquarters in Atlanta, in Chippewa County, they went hand in hand. According to the 1920 census, nearly 15.0 percent of Chippewa County residents were born in a foreign country, while a whopping 40.9 percent claimed at least one parent of foreign birth.[20] Industries such as logging, manufacturing, agriculture and railroads demanded large numbers of low-skilled and low-paid laborers. These positions were filled by immigrants from Germany, Norway, French Canada, Ireland, Poland and other countries in Scandinavia and Eastern Europe. While German and Norwegian Protestants assimilated more easily into the larger white,

Above: Immigrants from eastern Europe were frequent targets of Klan propaganda, circa 1926. *Author's collection.*

Opposite: Schedule for a major Wisconsin Klan event in 1926. *Author's collection.*

Anglo-Saxon, Protestant social structure, Catholic immigrants did not. They built their own churches and parochial schools, resided together in common neighborhoods and maintained their own cultural mores and traditions, including the consumption of alcohol.[21]

From the northern Klan's perspective, Jews and Roman Catholics were the greatest immediate threat to the United States. Imperial Wizard Evans wrote, "A large number among the vast hoard of immigrants who have reached our shores in the last thirty years have been Catholics…and Jews." He explained, "Protestant America must have time to teach these alien peoples the fundamental principles of human liberty before we permit further masses of ignorant, superstitious, religious devotees to come within our borders."[22] Jews were accused of manipulating the nation's monetary interests, while

Realm Klonvocation

Fond du Lac, Sept., 18th and 19th, 1926

Saturday forenoon Establishing Headquarters, Committee Work, Getting Acquainted and Setting up the meeting.

1:00 Community Singing................................V. E. HITCHCOCK

1:30 Introduction of the Grand Dragon of Wisconsin, Ralph Hammond.

2:00 Introduction of the Major Kleagle of the Women of the Ku Klux Klan, Mrs. Sara B. Bellows.

2:30 Great Titan of the Province, Dr. Daniel Woodward, Wisconsin Klan Problems.

3:00 Pat Malone, Klankraft and the Teachings of the Order.

3:30 Address by H. P. Peevey, Grand Klaliff.

4:00 Parade led by Fond du Lac Military Band.

5:00 Drill on the grounds by Milwaukee Drill Team.

EVENING PROGRAM

6:00 Music by Fond du Lac Military Band.

8:00 Address by Judge Orbinson of Indiana.

9:15 Naturalization of Klanswomen on the grounds in public ceremony illustrated by Fireworks.

SUNDAY PROGRAMS

10:00 Meetings of Grand Dragon and Officers at the Armory in Fond du Lac.

10:00 Meeting of Major Kleagle of the Women of the Ku Klux Klan and Kleagles in the tent on the grounds.

AFTERNOON

1:00 Address by Judge Orbinson to K-DUO Members and Candidates.

2:00 Both sections of the K-DUO Degree put on in full form in Armory. No one except Members and Candidates of the K-DUO Degree will be admitted to the Armory.

1:30 Sunday afternoon the full program will be under the auspices of the Woman's Organization. Several Klanswomen's drill teams, Tri-K Drills and Klanswomen's choruses with addresses will make an appropriate full Sunday afternoon program.

SUNDAY EVENING

8:00 The Pat Malone Campaign will resume work in regular form with his famous address; Wisconsin State Institutions. The Pat Malone meetings will continue on the Fond du Lac grounds, closing on September 26th, as per bills and other announcements.

All meetings on the Klan grounds in Fond du Lac are open to the public except the Kleagle's meeting in the tent Sunday forenoon. The tent will be closed to the public for two hours Sunday forenoon, but all other parts of the grounds are open to the public.

All meetings at the Armory are open only to K-DUO members and men making application for that Degree. The Great Titan will receive applications up to noon Sunday.

An admission of 25c will be charged at both grounds and the Armory. Children over eight years, 15c. Parking free during realm meeting.

Roman Catholics were thought to be planning an eventual overthrow of the United States. According to Evans, a Catholic, in particular, could never be a true American citizen, as the religion calls for the "monarchical idea that the individual is a subject…not a citizen." Unlike public schools, where Evans believed children were taught to think for themselves, he believed that parochial schools were established to "teach them what to think" and to act as an indoctrination "agent for the religion." In addition, the Pope wasn't just the religious leader of the Roman Catholic Church, he was also a political head of state for a sovereign country, Vatican City. Evans predicted that the pontiff was using immigration as a means to invade, populate and conquer the American continent from within. If this grandiose plot was true, Chippewa Falls was in serious peril, as it was situated on the frontlines of the war with a sizable and politically active Catholic population.[23]

4

STRANGERS IN THE NIGHT

The Klan Arrives in Western Wisconsin

As Klan mania spread throughout the United States, its arrival into the Chippewa Falls area, by comparison, seemed late. The first published acknowledgement of Klan activity in Chippewa Falls wasn't until January 30, 1924, when the *Eau Claire Leader* reported "Efforts to Organize a Klan" within the city. A Kleagle, or field organizer, had been rumored to be giving "select citizens" invitations to join.[24] Referenced in the newspaper as J.H. Neff, the organizer masked his true intentions by claiming he was in the area selling insurance. In less than two weeks, the Klan would burn its first cross within the city.

On Saturday, February 9, at nine o'clock at night, Nellie McGilvray of 415 North State Street reported seeing a burning cross in the field overlooking the Jacob Leinenkugel Brewing Company at the edge of a small grove of trees near Forest Hill Cemetery. The cross had been fashioned from "two by four timbers bolted together and wrapped in oil-soaked gunny sacks." The city's fire department decided that the blazing cross "could do no harm" and returned to the firehouse without extinguishing it. Witnesses reported seeing the "flaming cross plainly" from Bridge Street in the heart of the city's downtown. Within minutes of the arrival of the fire fighters, a large crowd had gathered to gossip. One witness counted twenty-five hooded men as they drove away in their automobiles, while another announced that the Klan had burned the cross to indicate the group's passing of the 500-membership mark. He added that it was 547 members to be exact.[25]

A members-only cross burning in Lake Hallie, Wisconsin. While the private ritual symbolized the light of Jesus Christ in an alien world, the intended meaning of a public burning varied, including membership milestones, general publicity and/or intimidation, circa 1927. *Author's collection.*

Eight days later, a second flaming cross was lit from the same vantage point. This one was made into an "X-shape" and stood twenty feet tall. The Klansmen lit the cross just as downtown crowds were leaving the Rex and Loop Theaters. The *Chippewa Herald* reported that a group of "small boys appeared as if by magic with piles of handbills," which included the letters KKK and a "picture of negro with grinning lips, staring eyes and disheveled hair." The leaflet read, "Kan't Ketch this Koon unless you see the Battery C Barrage of mirth, music and melody at the Junior High School Auditorium on February 20 and 21."[26] Within weeks, flaming crosses announcing Klan speaking events were seen throughout western Wisconsin, including the neighboring locales of Elk Mound, Cadott and Eau Claire. Within two years, the Klan boasted five independently chartered men's units in Chippewa County alone, including Bloomer Klan no. 11, Chippewa Falls Klan no. 12, Cornell Klan no. 13, Stanley Klan no. 14 and Jim Falls Klan no. 36.[27]

Kleagles like J.H. Neff were the secret ingredient to the national Klan's explosive growth in the 1920s, as they invaded assigned regions and stirred up any and all resentments that festered beneath the surface of a community. According to Catholic priest Peter Minwegen, the Klan came into Cornell and "worked like termites." They even distributed fake Knights of Columbus oath cards explaining how the Pope would soon give a universal "signal" for Catholics to engage in a simultaneous "killing, stabbing, or strangling of all their Protestant neighbors without exception."[28] This type of propaganda worked well for a Kleagle, who pocketed four dollars from a new initiate's first year dues of ten dollars. Regardless of which locale an organizer canvassed, the strategy was eerily repeated: identify which people caused apprehension among the white Protestant class; distribute propaganda materials designed to enhance extant social divisions; offer free membership to prominent citizens (clergymen, politicians and businessmen); and organize an initial meeting and membership induction ceremony. In the Chippewa Falls visit alone, Kleagle Neff earned $2,188 for the 547 new initiates ($40,000 by 2018 standards).

Neff's crowning organizational achievement in Chippewa County was the gigantic Klan spectacle that was held in the nearby city of Cornell. An estimated total of eighteen thousand spectators in more than four thousand cars swarmed the small logging city with thirteen hundred residents.[29] The program included speeches, a forty-piece Klan Band, carnival-style games and a parade containing more than five hundred robed and hooded Klansmen. Riding on one of the parade floats were robed Klanswomen from Chippewa Falls flanked by eighteen robed Klansmen on horseback. By evening's end, the throng had crossed the Chippewa River and held a naturalization ceremony for eight hundred new members.[30] The *Chippewa Herald* wrote that the event certainly relieved the city of its "mill-town monotony," or as one resident observed, it was "quite the biggest thing that ever happened in Cornell."[31]

5
WOMEN OF THE KU KLUX KLAN

The history of women within the national revival of the Ku Klux Klan is complicated. Under the initial design of the men's Klan in 1915, women were not allowed to join. As the Klan's popularity expanded, so did the desire among women to participate. To fill the female demand, several unaffiliated groups formed across the country, including the Ladies of the Invisible Empire (LOTIE) and Queens of the Golden Mask (QGM).[32] By 1922, the Knights of the Ku Klux Klan had changed their position on women due to financial considerations. Why limit dues payments to just one member of a family when a married couple would gladly pay for two?

Less than a year later, a power struggle ensued between Emperor William J. Simmons, now a symbolic figurehead, and the day-to-day leader, Imperial Wizard Dr. Hiram Evans. Simmons formed a women's group called Kamelia, and Evans followed suit with the Women of the Ku Klux Klan. Eventually, a court decided the fate of women within the Klan, as Simmons was ordered to "resign his rights, title, and interest" in both Kamelia and the men's Ku Klux Klan. Evans was now the standalone leader of the men's unit, and he had big financial goals in mind for the new WKKK.[33]

The Women of the Ku Klux Klan was incorporated on June 8, 1923, as a purely female-run organization designed to be separate from the men's Klan. Even the placement of their headquarters in Little Rock, Arkansas, was selected to discourage the meddling of the men's leadership in Atlanta.[34] The new women's organization sought to "bring together Protestant women for…practical politics and use of the ballot…advocate for the use of the English language…teach allegiance to the American Constitution and flag…and return the Bible to American public schools." It also called for "religious tolerance," but would oppose groups that taught the doctrine of "social equality of all races." The WKKK would also "encourage a study" of the "vital questions affecting the happiness of the home" and "work for the protection of the American home and the honor of American womanhood." Seen as the most essential ingredient of a safe, healthy and happy home life, the WKKK vehemently opposed the consumption of intoxicating liquors through their support of national and state Prohibition laws.

The newly formed WKKK also offered conservative women a path to increased social status. In a 1924 speech titled "American Women," the WKKK's national leader, Robbie Gill-Comer, made it clear that she believed God wanted men and women to stand as equals within the home and that Protestantism within the United States uniquely granted "the liberties, the rights, the opportunities, and the protection of womanly virtues." The Imperial Commander added, "I make bold to assert that it has never been the purpose of God that women should be the slave of men" and that every "American woman is a queen" of some degree.[35] She later wrote, "Our knees can be altars of patriotism…and our homes shrines of idealism where liberty can be fostered," as we will "vote with our men for right men, right programs, and right government."[36] To emulate this symbolism, Gill-Comer wore a diamond encrusted crown rumored to be valued at $30,000—nearly half a million dollars today.

On Monday, August 25, 1924, Klan organizer J.H. Neff held a "business meeting" for sixty Chippewa County Klanswomen at a home on Lake Wissota.[37] It is not known if Neff was trying to sign them up for Simmons's Kamelia or Evans's WKKK. If the Chippewa Falls women did organize as Kamelia prior to switching over to the WKKK, there are no documented records of that group's activities. The first documentation records of the Chippewa Falls chapter of the WKKK was a letter to the membership titled "Important Meeting—All meetings are important." Dated October 1, 1926, it announced that the WKKK's meeting place, or Klavern, was located "over Penney's Store" in downtown Chippewa Falls. Located at 101 North Bridge Street, the original J.C. Penney retail store was on the first floor of the city's iconic Metropolitan Block Building. On the third floor was a lodge room that was home to the local chapter of the national Knights of Pythias, a social club known for "Friendship, Charity, and Benevolence." In this golden age of fraternal orders, it was commonplace for groups like the Pythians

TO BE FORWARDED TO HEADQUARTERS

Form 100—J.F.H.

APPLICATION FOR CITIZENSHIP
IN THE
INVISIBLE EMPIRE

Women of the Ku Klux Klan
(Incorporated)

To Her Majesty the Imperial Commander of the Invisible Empire, Women of the Ku Klux Klan:

I, the undersigned, a native born, true and loyal citizen of the United States of America, being a white female Gentile person of temperate habits, sound in mind and a believer in the tenets of the Christian religion, the maintenance of White Supremacy and the principles of a "pure Americanism," do most respectfully apply for membership in the Women of the Ku Klux Klan through Klan No................., Realm of..............................

I guarantee on my honor to conform strictly to all rules and requirements regulating my "naturalization" and the continuance of my membership, and at all times a strict and loyal obedience to your constitutional authority and the constitution and laws of the fraternity, not in conflict with the constitution and constitutional laws of the United States of America and the States thereof. If I prove untrue as a Klanswoman I will willingly accept as my portion whatever penalty your authority may impose.

The required contribution accompanies this application.

Signed..Applicant

Endorsed by

Kl..

Kl..

Residence Address..

Business Address..

Date..192.....

The person securing this application must sign on top line above. NOTICE—Check the Address to which mail may be sent.

TO BE GIVEN TO APPLICANT

NOTICE

The sum of this donation MUST accompany application, if possible. Upon payment of same by applicant this certificate is made out and signed by person securing application, then detached and given to applicant, who will keep same and bring it with her when she is called, and then turn it in on demand in lieu of the cash.

DO NOT detach if donation is not paid in advance.

OFFICIAL CERTIFICATE OF DONATION

THIS CERTIFIES THAT..

has donated the sum of FIVE DOLLARS to the propagating fund of the

Women of the Ku Klux Klan (Inc.)

and same is accepted as such and as full sum of contribution entitling her to be received, on the acceptance of her application, under the laws, regulations and requirements of the Order, duly naturalized and to have and to hold all the rights, titles, honors and protection as a citizen of the Invisible Empire. She enters through the portal of Klan No. ...., Realm of..............................

Received in trust for the

WOMEN OF THE KU KLUX KLAN (INC.)

By Kl..

Date.., 192.....

A membership application for "citizenship" in the WKKK, circa 1924. *Author's collection.*

to rent their lodge rooms to Klan chapters throughout the United States.[38] For a veteran Klanswoman to maintain an active membership within the order, she would pay a recurring quarterly membership fee of $1.50. Of that, $0.70 was used to pay Klecktoken, or taxes, to both the imperial office ($0.45 to the national headquarters) and the realm office ($0.25 to the state headquarters). The remaining majority, $0.80 per member, was kept locally within the treasuries of each Klan unit.[39]

The letter to the membership went on to encourage the Klanswomen to "know the truth," regarding the actual happenings of the Ku Klux Klan's big Klonvocation held in the nation's capital, Washington, D.C. It also criticized the "hired press" for underreporting the total number of Kluxers who attended the spectacle. Citing results from headcounts by Klan-supporting media outlets "throughout the country," the letter placed the total number at more than 150,000, compared to the mainstream media's report of just 20,000.[40] As far as local coverage of the event, the *Eau Claire Leader*'s front-page story made no mention of attendance figures but focused on the Klonvocation's reelection of the Imperial Wizard of the men's Klan, Hiram Evans.[41]

It was also implied that the women of the Chippewa Falls Klan were organized well before their official incorporation into the WKKK, possibly as early as the spring of 1924. They were likely organized in one of the two major forerunners to the WKKK, either Ladies of the Invisible Empire or Kamelia. The WKKK financial records reveal that July 25, 1927, was the "date when the charter was delivered" by the national WKKK to the local Chippewa Falls unit. Similar to how the men's Klans were organized, a female Kleagle, or field organizer, from the state's WKKK headquarters in Milwaukee would have assisted in completing the paperwork to organize the Klavern.[42] A second letter to the membership had been addressed to the "Brothers & Sisters" of both Chippewa Falls Klan organizations. It opened with an aura of excitement, as they eagerly planned to construct a new Klavern away from downtown Chippewa Falls. "As our fine new Klavern is about completed we will soon move from our preset place of meeting, but when we go into our new abode, we will wish to go in there with the Spirit of Klandom in every member—Klanswomen, Klansmen, Juniors, and Tri-K's."[43]

Just a few years earlier, in 1923, the national WKKK had created the Junior Prep for adolescent boys and the Tri-K program for teenage girls as auxiliary programs to expand its appeal to everyone within the family.[44] While the

The Metropolitan Block (first on the right) was home to J.C. Penney Company and the Knights of Pythias (third-floor sign reads "K.O.P"). The WKKK used the K.O.P. Hall for an unspecified number of meetings, circa 1924. *Author's collection.*

letter in the Klan file did not specifically attest to how many children were enrolled in the youth programs, or even if they offered them unofficially to save on dues payments, it did advertise an upcoming banquet for the entire family. It read, "We have arranged this Father & Son and Mother & Daughter Banquet, which will be in the nature of a Rabbit Supper" for Monday evening, November 22, 1926. The letter encouraged all Klansmen and Klanswomen to bring their sons and daughters to "create new interest in the organization, especially in the Junior and Tri-K work."[45] The letter added, "What we all want to do is to keep our young people on the honest path to pure manhood and womanhood and if it can be done anywhere, it surely can be done in the teachings of the Ku Klux Klan."[46]

The Chippewa Falls Klan members viewed the youth auxiliary programs as significant additions to their order and viewed the participation of their children as essential to perpetuating their beliefs and values. The proceeds of everyone's fifty-cent admission fee would be placed in the "expense fund," and the profit would be used to construct the new Klavern in the nearby Township of Lake Hallie. From July 1927 to February 1931, the Grey Eagles of Chippewa Falls would hold fifty-eight total meetings within the Chippewa Falls and Lake Hallie area before their disbandment. This is their story.

PART II

THE MEETING MINUTES OF THE CHIPPEWA FALLS WKKK, 1927–31

The following pages include excerpts from a transcription of the hand-recorded minutes of the fifty-eight meetings the Chippewa Falls Women of the Ku Klux Klan held between August 1927 and February 1931. Each meeting, or Klonklave, included the following routine: An opening ritual, the singing of "America," a reading and acceptance of the prior meeting's minutes, financial updates, discussions on old business, the sharing of new business, a closing ritual and a recitation of the Lord's Prayer. Due to space limitations, each installment of the minutes has been condensed by omitting these repetitive commonalities. The excerpts that remain include the unique happenings and activities from each of the meetings.

In addition to the documents within the "Women of the Ku Klux Klan 14 (Chippewa Falls, Wis.), 1926–1931" file, supporting evidence came from newspaper archives, obituaries, census data, genealogical records, interviews and artifacts from public and private collections. The passage of time made interviews a significant challenge, as all of the members of the Chippewa Falls WKKK, along with their spouses, have passed away. Nearly all of their children have also died, leaving grandchildren and great-grandchildren as the remaining standard-bearers of family history. I have made contact with most of the members' surviving relatives.

Without exception, family members of the women have been both supportive and gracious. Most who helped with the project wanted to keep their contributions anonymous. All of the names used are real individuals.

One final adaptation deals with the name of the current Village of Lake Hallie. During the 1920s and '30s, the municipality was simply known as the Hallie Township. In referencing this prominent location throughout the book, I refer to it as the Township of Lake Hallie to strike a balance between the rural nature of its past (township) and its modern geographical name (Lake Hallie).

I

1927

Klonklave No. 1

August 8, 1927, Monday, 8:00 p.m.

The first documented Klonklave, or officially recorded business meeting, of the Chippewa Falls WKKK contained topics that ranged from the locally mundane to the nationally significant. Along with being authorized to purchase stationery for their Klavern, Excellent Commander Tess Trainer also enthralled members with highlights from the Klan's Wisconsin State Klonvocation, or annual state assembly.

Held at the Winnebago County Fairgrounds in Oshkosh, the Klonvocation was first publicly announced on the front page of the *Oshkosh Northwestern* under the headline "Expect Thousands at Gathering for Ku Klux Klan." An estimated six thousand Kluxers attended. The morning program was filled with speakers from the WKKK, including an opening speech by Imperial Representative Mary Jane Bishop, followed in late morning by an oration from the WKKK's Imperial Commander Mrs. Robbie Gill-Comer. Aside from offering nationally renowned orators—always a key ingredient to the Klan's recruitment success—the day was filled with "singing, band concert music, special selections by a bugle corps, and concluded with a massive fireworks display."[1]

While the morning program featured prominent WKKK figures, the afternoon was dominated by speakers from the men's KKK. The evening was capped off by the most anticipated speech of the gathering, a keynote address by Imperial Wizard Dr. Hiram Evans. In a front page article titled "Voters' Apathy Draws Fire of Klan Leader," the *Eau Claire Leader* reported that Evans declared 1927 as a "year known for religious controversy throughout the country" but most notably for the "political indifference of the people."[2] Referencing the presence of prominent Roman Catholics within United States politics, including the New York governor, who would be the future Democratic nominee for president, Al Smith, Evans railed against the lack of urgency among Protestants by asking the crowd two questions: "Can a good Roman Catholic be a good efficient American office holder?" and "Can Al Smith be a good loyal American, no matter what kind of Catholic he is?"[3]

Speaking to two thousand white-robed men and women, which was far short of the original advertised projections, Evans declared, "The national government cannot be firmly established until the question of church versus state is settled." Even though Evans acknowledged that the Roman Catholic Church was "entitled to the same rights as other religious bodies," he worried that the Catholic Church would "take precedence" over the government. He passionately argued that the campaign of the Klan was the "greatest battle" ever waged for American freedom.[4] Despite the emotional and heated rhetoric that came from the speakers, the *Eau Claire Leader* mentioned "no disturbances marked the proceedings."[5]

In addition to Excellent Commander Trainer's recap of the convention, the other noteworthy topic was Grace Fisher's report on the Klan's desire to extend its influence through the use radio broadcasting. As the Klavern's Night Hawk, or courier/messenger, Fisher's role was to orally convey all WKKK communications to the attending membership. This proposal to expand into radio reflected the strength the Klan had achieved over the years and proved how mainstream its ideology had become to Protestants.

Weeks earlier, the parent company of the *Fellowship Forum*, an anti–Roman Catholic publication that called itself "The World's Greatest Fraternal Newspaper," submitted an approval request to the Federal Radio Commission. Its goal was to purchase a radio station in Brooklyn, New York, and then transfer it to Washington, D.C. Publisher James Vance, a well-known Klan sympathizer, announced that the station would focus on the promotion of patriotism and civil government, and include other programming such as Christian songs, hymns, sermons and lectures about agriculture.[6]

Initially, media outlets were skeptical of the Klan's ability to get into radio. The *Eau Claire Leader* took glee in the fact that even though the Klan "should be allowed" to disseminate their hatred on the airwaves, the Federal Radio Commission already had three hundred applications for radio station requests with no "wave lengths" available for any of them. The newspaper reminded the Klan that it could fill out an application and take its rightful place at the end of the long line. The paper added, "That's the square deal. First come, first served."[7] However, as author Craig Fox explained in his book *Everyday Klansfolk*, it was the Klan who would have the last laugh, as they did succeed in entering radio broadcasting. Klan-centered content and messaging would be transmitted, in some form, all across the United States.[8]

As for Excellent Commander Trainer, who had just turned forty-six on August 1, the timing of her birthday around the Klonvocation carried an enhanced meaning. Born in 1881 in Richmond, Indiana, Tessie Leley Eley would become the most significant individual in the story of the Grey Eagles. As the daughter of a prominent Indiana doctor and with high school education, Trainer was literate.[9] Tess married her first husband, Boyd Bidwell, at eighteen and gave birth to her first and only child, Donald. For reasons not fully known, Tess and Boyd's marriage ended in January 1902, after two tumultuous years. Tess's lifelong crusade against alcohol was likely shaped during this failed union, as Boyd was known to have "troubles" with alcohol, as evidenced by a guilty plea for illegally selling booze to a minor on his record.[10]

While employed as a housekeeper in Fulton County, Indiana, and while raising her son as a single mother, Tess met her second husband, Frank Trainer.[11] After their marriage on November 28, 1906, Frank and Tess moved around the Midwest. As a result of his railroad profession, Frank kept the family's residency fluid. The Trainers lived in a plethora of cities, including Erie, Indiana, and Spencer and Wausau, Wisconsin. By the time the Trainers had moved to Chippewa Falls, Frank was employed as a telegraph operator for the Soo Line Railroad.[12]

Within a year of arriving in Chippewa Falls, the Trainers moved into a two-story house at 1136 Warren Street, located within a residential neighborhood overlooking the city's downtown on the East Hill. Once more commonly known as Catholic Hill, the East Hill featured two prominent religious buildings, Notre Dame Church and the original

The East Hill home of Frank and Tess Trainer. *Photo by John Kinville.*

The East Hill of Chippewa Falls is home to several prominent Roman Catholic buildings, including *(from left to right)* McDonell Memorial High School *(columns)*, Notre Dame Grade School, Notre Dame Church *(bell tower and cross)* and the parsonage, or clergy house, circa 1909. *Author's collection.*

McDonell Central Catholic High School.[13] According to many excerpts found within the archives of the *Chippewa Herald*, Tess hosted several ice cream socials in her front yard for the Ladies Aid of the Church of Christ. This is also where Tess watched her mother die of rheumatism while visiting from Indiana.[14]

By late 1930, Frank, Tess and Donald Trainer had moved to other side of the city's downtown valley to a home on West Mansfield Street. Known as the West Hill, where the prominent Protestants had historically lived, it was populated with mansions built by wealthy lumber barons from the 1880s. This move across the city would have been perceived as a sign of upward mobility for any working-class family of the time.[15]

In addition to being a wife and mother, Tess was also an avid follower of political issues. Above all, it was her passionate abhorrence of alcohol that propelled her to organize. Known locally as an ardent supporter of Prohibition, she often wrote letters to the editor of the *Eau Claire Leader* defending the Eighteenth Amendment, which banned the "manufacture, sale, and transportation of intoxicating liquors" between 1920 and 1933.[16] Her disdain for alcohol would continue long after the dissolution of the women's Klan, as she would become a leading officer in the local chapter of the Woman's Christian Temperance Union.

Feeling invigorated from a weekend of Klan patriotism, family celebration and Protestant empowerment, Tess went on to successfully lead her first all-female Klonklave.

The minutes are as follows:

- *Meeting called...followed by prayer*
- *Moved by Clara Lange, seconded by Flora Campbell...allow Tess Trainer 54¢ for stationery*
- *Grace Fisher...reading on the broadcasting station*
- *Tess Trainer...report of the Oshkosh, Wisconsin meeting...very well ordered...very interesting*
- *Program put on by the Orchestra at Jim Falls...they netted $38.40*
- *Members present—14*
- *Tess Trainer—Excellent Commander*
- *Henrietta Tracy—Kligrapp (Pro Tem)*[17]

KLONKLAVE NO. 2

August 22, 1927, Monday, 6:30 p.m.

In the two weeks since its first meeting, several Klan-related articles appeared prominently in the *Eau Claire Leader*. On August 9, four Alabamian Klansmen pled guilty to flogging a "farm youth," and each man received fines of $500 and six months in prison. While this story had seemingly no direct impact on the Grey Eagles, it represented the negative publicity that continually plagued the national Klan.[18]

Ten days later, the local paper reported a Wisconsin-related Klan altercation that took place at a men's Klavern some forty-five miles north of Chippewa Falls. After the Grand Dragon of the Barron, Wisconsin, Klan spoke, a traveling Klan evangelist named Pat Malone lambasted the local leader. Malone accused the local Grand Dragon of conspiring against him in a slander case.[19] Pat Malone, born Arthur Malone, was a shadowy and controversial figure in the history of the midwestern Ku Klux Klan. Known for his stirringly controversial speeches and costumed theatrical performances, Malone was an official Klan lecturer. He advertised himself as a former priest who possessed firsthand knowledge of the evils and perversions perpetuated by the Roman Catholic Church. Malone's fiery orations left his audiences both mesmerized and horrified. Many of his wildest tales involved accusations of improper sexual relationships between priests and nuns that resulted in secret childbirths, orphanages filled with illegitimate children and late-night abortions. Often told without much direct evidence, Malone teetered on the edge of violating Wisconsin's slander and libel laws.[20]

Just over a year before, in July 1926, Malone was arrested in Oconto Falls for claiming that the town's priest had likely fathered "eight or nine illegitimate children." After being tried in county court and found guilty of criminal slander, Malone was sentenced to a year in jail. In March 1927, the Wisconsin State Supreme Court ordered Malone to receive a new trial because it found that the lower court allowed evidence that was not related to his specific case. In early June, Malone reappeared in a Marinette County Court for his retrial and pled guilty. After receiving a $100 fine, Malone allegedly told a Wisconsin senator that "he was through with the Ku Klux Klan forever. He feels he was made the goat in the matter by the Klan and he stated that he will now proceed to make some startling exposures of the Klan." Malone's outburst inside the Barron Klavern revealed a significant internal rift among key figures of the Wisconsin men's Klan.[21]

Left: Arthur "Pat" Malone, Klan lecturer, reverend and propagandist, circa 1926. *Author's collection.*

Right: Malone's song book included songs such as "America," "Stand Up for Jesus" and "Oh, He Ain't Gonna Rule No More" (referencing the Pope). *Author's collection.*

Of all of the anti-Klan press in the area, the most bizarre story involved a man who claimed he had been terrorized by members of the WKKK. Referring to himself as a "coffee house representative" who was in Eau Claire on business, the unidentified man told the Eau Claire County sheriff that three carloads of robed women followed him on a ninety-five-mile trip from La Crosse to Eau Claire. He reported that during a few of his restaurant stops, the women snuck into the back of each business and attempted to kill him by poisoning his coffee. Even though the man seemed "perfectly rational" on all other subjects, Sheriff Tom Anderson observed that he had a "great aversion to women." The strange man confessed to the sheriff by claiming, "Catholic women were just as bad as Klanswomen because once a Catholic woman had permitted herself to be overpowered by Klanswomen who were after him." The man stayed one night in the county jail and was released the next day.[22]

As for the August 22 meeting, it is revealed that the Chippewa Falls Women of the Ku Klux Klan used a committee system to delegate tasks within the Klavern. The kitchen committee prepared a meal or snack for each meeting. Referred to by the women as a "lunch," the meal was either served before or after the official meeting. The program committee was responsible for scheduling fundraisers and other events, while the Klokan committee was in charge of vetting new applicants.

The meeting notes are as follows:

- *Connell...chairman of Kitchen Committee…*
- *Lange...chairman of the Program Committee…*
- *Klokan Committee...authorized to get a frame for our charter…*
- *Mildred Peterson…home from hospital, each member asked to send birthday card*
- *Members present—14*
- *Tess Trainer—Excellent Commander*
- *Henrietta Tracy—Kligrapp (Pro Tem)*[23]

KLONKLAVE NO. 3

September 7, 1927, Wednesday, 8:30 p.m.

By the third meeting of the Chippewa Falls WKKK, the *Eau Claire Leader* had learned more about the man who claimed to be a target of WKKK terrorism. It was reported that he was transported 175 miles south to the Mendota Mental Health Institute in Madison. The Eau Claire sheriff explained that the man was a physical and mental wreck who was needlessly worried that women from the Klan would "pounce upon him" if he were to fall asleep in his jail cell. He was convinced that the women were angry with him for stealing a cow.[24] Despite his obvious need for professional psychiatric care, the newspaper seemed puzzled about how this man was found with certificates and bank receipts that showed him to be worth more than $31,000 ($431,000 by 2018 standards).

As for the September 7 meeting, several events made it memorable for the members present. First, the members of Klan no. 14 received a note of thanks for their financial backing in the *Fellowship Forum* newspaper's effort to create a pro-Klan radio station outside of Washington, D.C. The allure of broadcasting Klan messaging and propaganda with state-of-the-art radio technology was too promising of a recruitment tool for the Grey Eagles to ignore.

A second major development was the vote to establish the Grey Eagles as financial partners in the construction of a new Chippewa Falls Klavern building. Whether the idea originated from themselves or was offered by their male counterparts is unclear. The minutes suggest that while the women would control 49 percent interest in the newly constructed Klavern, the controlling 51 percent interest would presumably be retained by the men's unit.[25]

While it proves that the men wanted to reinforce gender roles and reserve majority control on the key decisions related to the project, this plan also illustrates how crucial the women's Klan was to the project's success. When the women agreed to take on the financial responsibility of the project's total cost ($13,800 in 2018 valuation), they established themselves as potent and equal stakeholders.

Being 49 percent owners of the Klavern came with enormous financial obligations, which would need to be acquired through rampant fundraising. One of the most popular, recurring and profitable fundraisers that the women hosted were "box socials." Popular in Canada and the United States in the early 1900s, box socials were gatherings where male participants would bid on a cardboard box filled with a meal or an assortment of food items. The women of the Klan would create these boxes anonymously so that the men could not tell which box was put together by which woman. The bidding process was usually accompanied by hints and clues or teasing and joking by other participants. Afterward, the winning bidders would receive the contents of the box, which they would eat with the woman who put the items together. These socials were generally effective as fundraisers because they mixed mystery, humor and fellowship.

Official embossed seal of the Grey Eagles of Chippewa Falls. *Author's collection.*

The urgency and enthusiasm the women must have felt to raise money for the new Klavern was evident by the plethora of events they planned. A theatrical performance was scheduled for September 24, a repeat of a prior year's father and son/mother and daughter banquet was scheduled for October

12 and a Thanksgiving dinner was discussed for November. Thinking about the more practical side of constructing a building, the women agreed that each member should donate a sack of concrete for the Klavern's new floor.[26]

In the meantime, the women present attempted to establish their identity by brainstorming a name for their individual Klan. Names like Golden Rods, Night Hawks, Oak Leaf Circle and All-American League were debated. In the end, the women of Klan no. 14 settled on the Grey Eagles.[27]

The meeting notes are as follows:

- *Klanswoman Hansen read a letter of thanks from the Fellowship Forum for $7.00 sent to the Radio Fund…*
- *Excellent Commander explained why we ought to take 49% interest in the Klavern, amounting to $980.00. Motion…by Hansen, seconded by Campbell…carried*
- *…box social for Saturday…*
- *Play to be put on…24th of September, admission..15¢ and 35¢*
- *Father and Son—Mother and Daughter banquet of chicken dinner… October 12th, plate—50¢*
- *County meeting..held at Jim Falls, September 20th*
- *Suggested to have Thanksgiving dinner at the Klavern…*
- *Campbell suggested naming our club "Golden Rod," "Night Hawks," "Oak Leaf Circle" or "All American League"*
- *…suggested we get new Constitutions, accepted*
- *We were asked…about donating a sack of cement, each member donating one for a new floor in the Klavern*
- *Song—Alone by Trainer and Lange*
- *Members present—15*
- *Tess Trainer—Excellent Commander*
- *Clara Lange—Kligrapp (Pro Tem)*[28]

KLONKLAVE NO. 4

September 21, 1927, Wednesday, 8:30 p.m.

In the days leading up to the September 21 meeting, a Voice of the People submission in the *Eau Claire Leader*, criticized the Ku Klux Klan organization. The author included a copy of a *New York Times* article referencing the views of a former U.S. senator from Mississippi. In response, he wrote, "The clipping…is good reading. It is my opinion that there is more good Americanism in Honorable John Sharp Williams' little finger than there is in a million full grown so-called progressives of the US, including those of Wisconsin."[29]

In the *New York Times* article, Senator John Sharp Williams blasted the Klan as unworthy of its name. Citing the original post–Civil War KKK as a group of "decent men" who were dedicated to the preservation of "law and order," he claimed that the original hooded order welcomed Roman Catholics and Jews into its ranks. Senator Williams added, "Preaching intolerance of Roman Catholics and Jews, and adding to it negro baiting, is surely not a high-standard of citizenship, to express it most mildly." He argued, "If Jews, Catholics, or negroes are dangerous to the American Republic, the danger can be made clear by public discussion. But of course, they are not dangerous. The very suggestion is ridiculous."[30]

In the following day's edition of the *Eau Claire Leader*, an article from Columbus, Georgia, featured the disappearance of a former Wisconsin Episcopal pastor. Local Columbus authorities originally believed that the Reverend Willis Jordan was a victim of the area Ku Klux Klan. In fact, another Columbus reverend who admitted to being a member of the KKK was held on charges of kidnapping. It was later revealed that the Klan had nothing to do with Reverend Jordan's disappearance.[31] He was found alive in North Carolina, having abandoned his family for another woman.

Not all of the press was bad, though. In the regional news brief section of the September 14 *Eau Claire Leader*, it was reported that "Mr. Pritchard and children motored to Menomonie (WI.), Sunday to attend the Klan meeting, with the Knapp unit putting on the program."[32] Once again, the Klan had proven to be an enjoyable outlet for Protestant families in the 1920s.

In spite of the state and national media reports that seemed to show the Klan's popularity fading, the Grey Eagles of the WKKK were just getting started. This particular installment of the minutes opens with the much-anticipated moment when the members received the shipment containing their Klavern's altar set. Consisting of an altar flag (small American flag), the Holy Bible, a chalice to hold water, a ritual sword and a "Fiery Cross" (cross-shaped candle holder), the arrival of the altar set nearly completed the items needed to carry out the rituals of the Klavern.[33]

Meanwhile, the women continued their feverish pace to raise money to fund the 49 percent partnership in the new Klavern project by hosting an upcoming pie social and chicken dinner banquet. The hectic pace

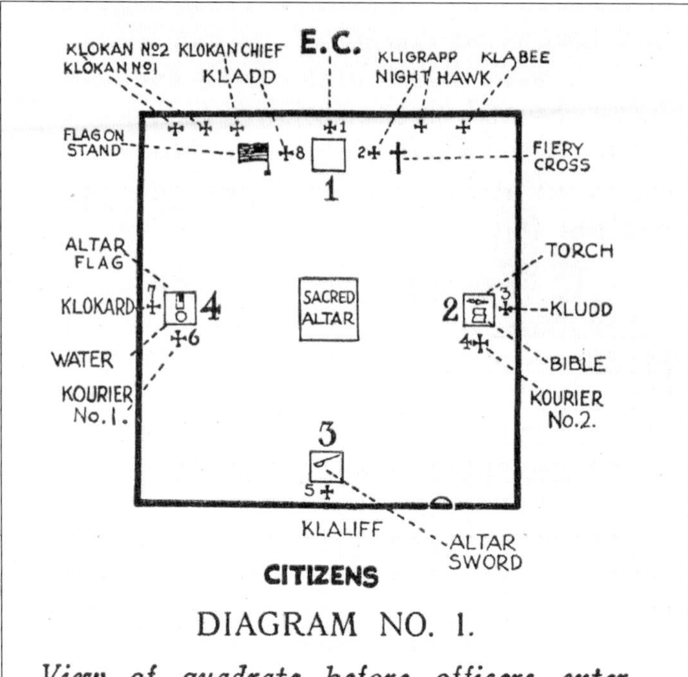

Floor plan for the inside of a WKKK Klavern. *WKKK Kloran, 1927.*

presumably left them with little time to perfect their theatrical performance, so they postponed the event.

The meeting notes are as follows:

- *...new Altar Set was unpacked, admired, and placed...*
- *...pie social Saturday evening, September 24th*
- *...postponement of the play until November...*
- *The chicken supper banquet for October 12th was talked over...Mae Connell...in charge of the kitchen until...October 12th.*
- *Members Present—14*
- *Tess Trainer—Excellent Commander*
- *Adella Ellsworth—Kligrapp*[34]

Klonklave No. 5

October 5, 1927, Wednesday, 8:30 p.m.

The October 5 meeting was dominated by the sorrowful news of the death of Klanswoman Hannah Waller of Chippewa Falls. According to her obituary, Mrs. Waller died two days prior as a result of a "week's illness and an operation for a tumor." The forty-four-year-old Waller left behind a husband, listed as T.P. Waller, as well as one son, Marvin. After funeral services at the Waller home, located at 315 West Elm Street in Chippewa Falls, a follow-up service was held at Our Savior's Lutheran Church in Eau Claire, with burial of her remains in Northside Lutheran Cemetery.[35]

Both the men's and women's Ku Klux Klan organizations were known for having ornate funerary and burial rituals, as outlined in the WKKK's manuals titled "Funeral Service and Burial Service."[36] Aside from the flowers that were sent by her fellow Grey Eagles, there is no definitive evidence that the women of Klan no. 14 conducted their own funeral service at either the home or grave site of Klanswoman Waller.[37]

In addition to the death of Waller, continued fundraising efforts dominated the agenda. It was agreed that "a sale," presumably of donated family and household items, would be added to the Thanksgiving Day event.

On an organizational level, Excellent Commander Tess Trainer wanted each member of the Grey Eagles to have her own personal copy of the national WKKK's most recent version of the constitution and laws booklet. Created and adopted by national delegates at the WKKK's First Imperial Klonvocation in St. Louis, Missouri, these booklets laid out the configuration of the entire national organization. Like any other standard constitution, the document addressed the basic foundational structure and principles of the order, such as "objects and purposes, officers and their duties, paraphernalia and regalia, geographical jurisdictions, offenses and punishments, and specific details outlining the amendment process."[38]

What is written within the preamble of the WKKK Constitution, however, might explain why Excellent Commander Trainer was so eager to have her Grey Eagles obtain one. The preamble stated, "We, the members of this Order, citizens and probationers of the Invisible Empire, Women of the Ku Klux Klan…declare this constitution of the WKKK, in lieu of the original prescript of the Knights of the Ku Klux Klan, as the supreme law of this Society, and pledge our voice, our loyalty, our womanhood, and our sacred honor to enforce the same."[39] Certified with the printed signature of Imperial Commander Robbie Gill-Comer near the end of the booklet, this document declared the WKKK as completely separate from the men's organization, whose constitution had initially provided a template for the women's order to consider upon their initial chartering in 1923.[40]

The meeting notes are as follows:

- *Motion...by Tracy, seconded by Hansen to take $2.50 from general fund for flowers for deceased member Hannah Waller...carried*
- *...order 12 constitutions*
- *Moved by Fisher, seconded by Clark...dinner and sale on Thanksgiving Day...carried*
- *Several letters read...from our State Lady, Klanswoman Bishop... plans to reinstate delinquent members*
- *Excellent Commander gave notice...afternoon tea at Klanswoman Earl's...*
- *Members Present—11*
- *Tess Trainer—Excellent Commander*
- *Adella Ellsworth—Kligrapp*[41]

KLONKLAVE NO. 6

October 19, 1927, Wednesday, 8:30 p.m.

Two weeks after the Grey Eagles lost fellow Klanswoman Hannah Waller to cancer, the October 19 meeting suggested that the Klavern returned to normal. The members meticulously planned their upcoming Thanksgiving fundraiser banquet, which was scheduled for Halloween. The event was to feature a rabbit dinner, thrift sale and Fish Pond game for the kids. Klanswomen Clara Lange, Myrtle Hansen and Belle Nelson volunteered to decorate the Klavern, while Klanswomen Henrietta Tracy, Josie Wallace and Emma Shaffer organized the thrift sale.

Meanwhile, Klanswoman Mary Card volunteered to oversee a game called Fish Pond. Originally released by the Milton Bradley Corporation in 1909, the Fish Pond board game consisted of six cardboard fish on wooden stands, two wooden dowel fishing rods with wire hooks attached to strings and a cardboard box featuring a colorful pond scene. According to the directions, each player was allowed one minute to hook and catch as many fish as they could. After playing five complete rounds, the player with the highest grand total of fish won the game.[42]

The attending members had good reason to think that the Thanksgiving event would be a success, considering that their last chicken dinner netted a profit of $58.69 ($828.00 by 2018 standards). More successful events like these would ensure that the Grey Eagles would live up to their partnership in the new Klavern building.

Unfortunately, the energy and excitement from the fundraising efforts was dampened by the resignation of another officer. Two meetings prior, Klanswoman Eva Arnold had resigned as the Klavern's second Klokan, or investigator. During this meeting on October 19, the Klavern's Klabee, or treasurer, also resigned. Filling all of the officer positions on a biweekly basis became a recurring problem for the Grey Eagles.[43]

As for Excellent Commander Tess Trainer's "talk on current events," several front-page headlines in the *Eau Claire Leader* would have spurred a Klanswoman's interest. As they were firmly against labor unions, the October 18 article titled "Supreme Court Affirms Ruling Against Unions—Injunctions against United Mine Workers Held Legal—Large Pittsburgh Coal Company Announces Cut in Wage Rate" likely would have created adulation among the women in the Klavern.[44]

The meeting notes are as follows:

- *Motion...by Strong, seconded by Fisher to have our Thanksgiving sale on the evening of the rabbit supper...October 31...carried*
- *Committee appointed...have charge of rabbit supper...*
- *Fish Pond—Klanswoman Card*
- *Sale Committee—Tracy, Wallace, Shaffer*
- *Decoration Committee—Lange, Hansen, Nelson*
- *Report of the chicken supper from October 12th given*
- *Klabee, Amanda Hermann, resigned. Excellent Commander appointed Henrietta Tracy to fill...*
- *Excellent Commander gave talk on current events*
- *Members Present—13 and 1 visitor*
- *Tess Trainer—Excellent Commander*
- *Henrietta Tracy—Kligrapp (Pro Tem)*[45]

KLONKLAVE NO. 7

November 2, 1927, Wednesday, 8:30 p.m.

With the Thanksgiving Day dinner just two days before, the meeting minutes reveal the Grey Eagles to be fundraising juggernauts. A net profit of $48.04 ($678.00 by 2018 standards) was made from the thrift sale, kid's game and rabbit supper. Since the event coincided with Halloween, the women added a children's candy counter to the festivities.

Emboldened by their success from the rabbit supper, the members energetically planned their next event for just nine days later. Similar to the box social earlier in the year, this next dinner would feature baskets instead of cardboard boxes. In addition to the baskets, grab-bags filled with popcorn, peanuts and candy would be available for children. This fundraiser would be hosted at the farm of Klanswoman Ruth E. Peterson in the Township of Lake Hallie.[46]

Located several miles south of the city of Chippewa Falls, the Peterson farm was owned by sixty-one-year-old Carl Peterson. Officially documented in the 1930 federal census, Carl was listed as "head" of household, while both of his adult children, Mildred and Alvin, also maintained residency on his farm. Sharing the living space on the property were Alvin's wife, Ruth,

Picnic-style box social near Chippewa Falls, circa 1927. *Author's collection.*

A Grey Eagle prepares food near Chippewa Falls, circa 1927. *Author's collection.*

their two young sons and two lodgers who were listed as farm "helpers" (one male and one female).[47]

Born Ruth Elizabeth Modin on July 29, 1897, Ruth married Alvin Peterson at Immanuel Lutheran Church in Eau Claire. On the night of this meeting, the Petersons were one month away from celebrating their five-year wedding anniversary. Twenty-nine-year-old Ruth was balancing the responsibilities of a young marriage while raising two boys in a full household and volunteering her free-time to Klan no. 14. Needless to say, her fellow Grey Eagles accepted the invitation and were eager to grow their chapter's fundraising chest for the new Klavern building.[48]

On a somber note, the minutes reveal that the father of a recently reinstated member, Klanswoman Laurel Waller, had passed away. Advertised in his obituary as a "survivor of the logging days," Everett S. Parker's remains had to be transported back to Chippewa Falls from Kenosha, roughly 290 miles away. Continuing the trend of showing compassion for a fellow member during a time of sorrow, the Grey Eagles sent flowers to his funeral. These funds, which would usually come from a segregated reserve called the "Sunshine Fund," were normally raised with the members purchasing a "lunch" meal that was served before or after the meetings.

As it pertains to the WKKK organization, this meeting also revealed the women's strong desire to be connected to the state and national units.

Excellent Commander Tess Trainer directed the creation of a bylaws committee and scheduled a "special meeting" to be held on the following Wednesday, specifically to read information bulletins from the state and national WKKK. Aside from just wanting to hold fundraisers and provide sunshine to members in need, the Grey Eagles were loyal foot soldiers who were restless in their desire to turn the United States into the white, Protestant and alcohol-free utopia they thought it could be.[49]

The meeting notes are as follows:

- *Bill of $2.50 for flowers for Mrs. Waller's father, Everett S. Parker... presented. Moved by Hansen, seconded by Tracy...carried*
- *Report of sale and rabbit supper given:*
- *Sale proceeds—$19.68*
- *Fish Pond—$5.00*
- *Candy Counter—$1.11*
- *Supper net—$22.25*
- *Grand Total—$48.04*
- *Proceeds...applied to building fund, moved by Clark, seconded by Shaffer...carried*
- *Klanswoman Ellsworth suggested...popcorn, peanuts, and candy for next grab-bag, moved by Clark, Hansen seconded...*
- *Klanswoman Ruth Peterson...invitation to have basket social at her home...Friday evening November 11th...*
- *Committee appointed to draw up bylaws. Smock and Hansen, Excellent Commander and Kligrapp as helpers...special meeting for November 9th, to hear bulletins read...*
- *Members Present—16*
- *Tess Trainer—Excellent Commander*
- *Adella Ellsworth—Kligrapp*[50]

KLONKLAVE NO. 8 (SPECIAL)

November 9, 1927, Wednesday, 8:30 p.m.

During the days preceding the "special Klonklave" scheduled by Excellent Commander Tess Trainer, the *Eau Claire Leader* reported a story featuring a "rumor from well-defined sources" that Reverend Daniel Woodward was thinking about running in the Republican primary for the 1928 United States Senate race. This would not be Woodward's first attempt to win a Senate seat. He was currently a Protestant Oshkosh minister who once served as the warden of the Wisconsin State Penitentiary at Waupun.[51] In 1925, following the untimely death of Republican progressive and politically revolutionary United States senator Robert "Fighting Bob" LaFollette, a special election was held to fill the vacant seat. Throughout the 1920s, Wisconsin was a stronghold for the Republican Party. Winning the primary was usually more significant than the general election itself, where the Democrat rarely had a chance. Woodward, who was openly supportive of and officially backed by the Ku Klux Klan, ran on a platform of "complete and unqualified endorsement of the Republican Party and the administration of President Calvin Coolidge."[52] What complicated Woodward's rise, and thus limited the Ku Klux Klan's overall political success in Wisconsin, was the popularity and dominance of the Lafollette progressive wing of the state's Republicans.

Known for their attacks against political corruption and predatory corporations, the LaFollette faction favored solutions that were viewed as advantageous to the individual worker, seemingly regardless of a worker's ethnic, religious or racial background. From the Klan's perspective, the Lafollette faction's platform was complicated and problematic. On one hand, Klan members were drawn to the ideals of corruption-free government and isolationist foreign policy. On the other hand, the faction avoided a firm position on the divisive issue of Prohibition, choosing instead to focus on the economic issues it believed were the underlying causes of alcoholism.

Most alarming, however, were the personal and political views that members of the Lafollette family aimed at the Ku Klux Klan organization. In a *New York Times* article in 1924, Senator Robert Lafollette Sr. was quoted saying, "I am unalterably opposed to the evident purposes of the secret organization known as the Ku Klux Klan…and any discrimination between races, classes and creeds." The family patriarch insisted that the real issue behind groups like the Klan was needing to break the political control of the corporate "power of private monopoly." While Lafollette was honestly and legitimately anti-Klan, he was also mindful of its power in Wisconsin.[53]

The pro–Ku Klux Klan Republican candidate, Daniel Woodard, was trounced in the state primary. Losing handily to the late senator's son, thirty-year-old Robert M. Lafollete Jr., Republican primary voters overwhelmingly wanted "Young Bob" to carry on the progressive tradition by filling the seat of their beloved "Fighting Bob." Woodward's official Klan support, along with his call for strict adherence to the enforcement of Prohibition laws, was no match for the people's nostalgic and political desire for another Lafollette. For Woodward, it had been a frustrating campaign. Speaking at the Ku Klux Klan State Klonvocation at the county fairgrounds in Madison, where more than one thousand Klansmen were in attendance, Woodward blamed the press for burying his candidacy by not covering him as much as his opponent.[54] Although the media did acknowledge Woodward's third-place finish, anti-Klan Lafollette received a resounding 55 percent of the primary vote. Meanwhile, the Klan-backed Woodward finished with a paltry 13 percent.[55] In the end, Lafollette would go on to easily defeat his general election opponents, receiving more than 67 percent of the total vote.[56]

If the Grey Eagles of Klan no. 14 were excited about another campaign by Daniel Woodward, in which he would face off against young Lafollete in 1928, the women made no mention of it within the minutes. For this special Klonklave, the task was to select a representative to attend to the WKKK's State Klorero, or state convention, in Milwaukee. While only six members of the Grey Eagles were in attendance, who they would choose to be their state representative was a forgone conclusion. Excellent Commander Trainer, by far the most qualified and educated within the details of Klankraft, was a logical choice. The members preauthorized Trainer to spend the generous sum of $10 for her expenses ($141 by 2018 standards), with all unspent funds to be returned to the Klavern.

The rest of the minutes reveal a coeducational program. While no evidence remains to divulge the context from the program itself, the "ladies were gratefully received by the men," adding to the body of evidence that the Grey Eagles continued to increase their cultural standing within the eyes of their male counterparts.

The meeting notes are as follows:

- *The question of sending a delegate to the Klorero in Milwaukee, Friday, November 18th, discussed...decided. Motion...by Fisher, seconded by Bollom to allow $10.00 from general fund for Excellent Commander's expenses...if anything is left...to be returned...*
- *Readings by Lange, Smock, and Trainer given...*
- *Ladies...united with the men's order to give their educational program... were gratefully received*
- *After the meeting soup served*
- *Members Present—6*
- *Tess Trainer—Excellent Commander*
- *Tess Trainer—Kligrapp (Pro Tem)*[57]

Klonklave No. 9

November 16, 1927, Wednesday, 8:30 p.m.

Leading up to their ninth Klonklave, the Klan's press coverage in western Wisconsin continued to be abrasive. An editorial published in the *Merrill Herald*, and reprinted by the *Eau Claire Leader*, posed that members of the KKK seemed to lack the ability to think for themselves. The newspaper added, "Highly educated people no doubt have joined the Ku Klux Klan without stopping to think to consider what such a secret organization would naturally lead to. Thinking men and women whether 'educated' or not have not joined the Kluxers."[58] Despite the ongoing public criticism of the Klan statewide, mostly as a result of their anti–Roman Catholic views, the minutes from the November 16 meeting revealed a local organization that, on paper, appeared to be unfazed.

On the fundraising front, the Grey Eagles continue their prowess. The basket social held at the farm of Ruth Peterson netted a respectable $30.75 ($434.00 by 2018 standards). This success spurred the group to initiate plans to hold another similar event, this time at the home of Klanswoman Emma Shaffer, which was located seven miles north of Chippewa Falls in the Township of Eagle Point.

After witnessing the success of the Peterson family's fundraiser, forty-one-year-old Klanswoman Emma Shaffer was eager to contribute. The Shaffer family farm, like the Peterson's, was a crowded homestead. Along with Emma and her husband, Charles, the Shaffers housed their two children, Earl and Ester, and Emma's younger brother Adolph. Emma was a dedicated parishioner at First Methodist Church in Chippewa Falls and was eager to help her Klan raise money for their new Klavern.[59]

The other women present at the Klonklave found it was refreshing to see Emma offer her services. Like Ruth Peterson before her, Emma never served as an officer during the roughly five-year timespan of Klan no. 14. As with any other fraternity or sorority that conducts oral ritual activities, role assignments that involve speaking parts leave many members too intimidated to volunteer. Box socials and other fundraising dinners provided a more attractive way for less vocally confident members to contribute to the rest of the Klan.

In addition to scheduling the next fundraiser, the Grey Eagles also conducted an audit of their expenditures, planned future installment payments on the new Klavern building and shared the fundraising credit

WOLVERINE WOMEN

VOL. I. GRAND RAPIDS, MICHIGAN, APRIL, 1928. No. 1

OUR REALM BULLETIN.

I took up the matter with the Imperial Commander relative to financing this Bulletin. She most heartily approved the Bulletin and the sending to each and every member a copy, and suggested that as Realm Commander I should send out a Realm Edict to each Klan to the effect that each Organization should immediately lay plans to establish a News Bulletin Sinking Fund in each Klan by any method the local Organization saw fit to adopt. She suggested that it could be created by a Silver Shower, Baked Goods Sales, Bazars, Dinners, Plays or something of this nature and then there would be at all times a sufficient amount of money to send in for this Bulletin in advance. Our Imperial Commander also suggested as the money was received for the papers that the Realm establish a Sinking Fund.

These papers as published at present will cost a fraction under five cents (5c) each, but it will cost us considerable to mail them and we are expecting the very probable necessity of sometimes during the campaign year ahead of us the need to send out a larger bulletin. We are hoping to have a little extra in the Realm News

MEMORIAL.

MRS. ALTA N. FULCHER.

First issue of the Michigan WKKK's monthly bulletin, circa 1928. *Author's collection.*

equally with the men's unit. Most importantly, from a meeting standpoint, the women of Klan no. 14 voted to "change our meeting place for the winter and meet at the different homes."[60] Rather than continue to meet in the Knights of Pythias Lodge in downtown Chippewa Falls, the women chose to enjoy the warmer and cozier confines of one another's homes. The tradeoff was likely a loss of Klavern privacy, as family members could easily interrupt or eavesdrop on the rituals and proceedings of the women's meetings.

Ending on yet another somber note, the Women of the Ku Klux Klan found themselves honoring the memory of a well-respected Klanswoman who had died in neighboring Michigan. Alta Fulcher, a prominent national speaker, had passed away at the age of fifty-seven. Known for her fiery and inspiring lectures on citizenship, immigration and support for prohibition, Fulcher was a vigorous and tenacious supporter of women's suffrage. She was adamant that women use their collective power to show interest in their communities—often using the analogy of a woman tending to a garden—to control the outcome of political and social issues of the day. As a ranking officer within the Woman's Christian Temperance Union (WCTU), Fulcher was known for her anti-alcohol stance and her desire for a home of "one language, one flag, one country, America for Americans."

In many ways, particularly for Excellent Commander Tess Trainer, Fulcher represented everything a conservative woman would want to be in the 1920s: talented, confident, patriotic and empowered.[61]

The meeting notes are as follows:

- *Report of basket social held at the Peterson's...total receipts $28.95*
- *A report of the receipts/expenses...from January 1 to November 1 was received from the men's order…*
- *Balance…$546.66*
- *Ladies received ½…apply...building fund*
- *Motion...by Clark, seconded by Earl...$50.00 from general fund... turn over to...building fund…carried*
- *After discussion, motion...by Hansen, seconded by Fisher...have box social and grab-bag…November 26th, Shaffer extended an invitation...at her home…carried*
- *...decided to change meeting place for the winter and meet at the different homes…*
- *Telegram…death of Mrs. Alta Fulcher, national speaker of... Michigan…Excellent Commander asked to send sympathy and regrets…*
- *Members Present—12*
- *Tess Trainer—Excellent Commander*
- *Adella Ellsworth—Kligrapp*[62]

Klonklave No. 10

November 30, 1927, Wednesday, 8:30 p.m.

The first winter meeting hosted away from the downtown Chippewa Falls Klavern was held at the home of Grace Fisher. Klanswoman Fisher was a farmer's wife who resided in the neighboring Township of Lake Hallie. Born Grace Fritzinger in 1880, she married George Fisher when she was twenty-one. Unlike the marriages of the Petersons and Shaffers, the eighteen-year age difference between Grace and George was significant. They were devout members of Hallie Methodist Evangelical Church and had a twenty-three-year-old who lived with them, Alvin, who was a truck driver for the Standard Oil Company.[63] Fisher was regarded as one of the most reliable members within the Klan, as she maintained one of the most consistent Klonklave attendance records.

Building on recent fundraising successes, the "box social and grab-bag" hosted by Emma Shaffer netted an impressive $33.05 ($466.00 by 2018 standards). Once again, the proceeds were applied to the building fund, with both the men and women receiving equal credit. Moving forward, however, it was understood that the women would keep half of the proceeds in their own treasury. This appears to be a sign that they were ahead of schedule for raising the funds to build the new Klavern and would begin to accumulate a nest egg for their own chapter.

One of the most revealing entries in this set of minutes was the information regarding the statewide numbers for the WKKK's membership. The entire Wisconsin Realm of the order was geographically divided into two provinces, a western block and an eastern block. Province no. 1, which contained the counties on the eastern side of Wisconsin, included most of the state's major population centers, including Green Bay (Brown), Madison (Dane), Kenosha (Kenosha), Milwaukee (Milwaukee), Racine (Racine) and Waukesha (Waukesha). Province no. 2, which contained the counties on the western side of the state, was decidedly more rural. The key population centers were Superior (Douglas), Chippewa Falls (Chippewa), Menomonie (Dunn), Eau Claire (Eau Claire), La Crosse (La Crosse) and Hudson (St. Croix). According to an entry in the minutes, the state realm of the WKKK reported that there were twenty-eight chartered women's Klans in Wisconsin, each with fewer than one hundred members.[64] It can be deduced that the number of statewide WKKK members exceeded no more than twenty-eight hundred

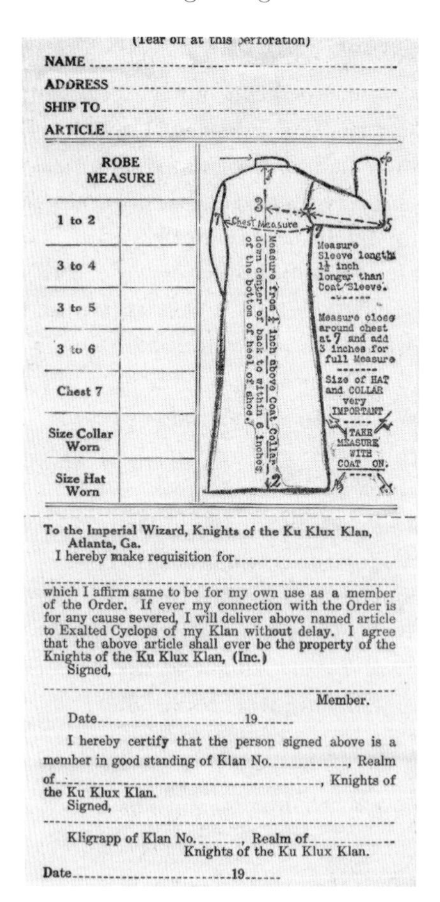

(Tear off at this perforation)

NAME ....

ADDRESS ....

SHIP TO..

ARTICLE ....

ROBE MEASURE	
1 to 2	
3 to 4	
3 to 5	
3 to 6	
Chest 7	
Size Collar Worn	
Size Hat Worn	

To the Imperial Wizard, Knights of the Ku Klux Klan, Atlanta, Ga.

I hereby make requisition for..

which I affirm same to be for my own use as a member of the Order. If ever my connection with the Order is for any cause severed, I will deliver above named article to Exalted Cyclops of my Klan without delay. I agree that the above article shall ever be the property of the Knights of the Ku Klux Klan, (Inc.)

Signed,

.... Member.

Date..........................19......

I hereby certify that the person signed above is a member in good standing of Klan No.............., Realm of.., Knights of the Ku Klux Klan.

Signed,

....

Kligrapp of Klan No........, Realm of.............. Knights of the Ku Klux Klan.

Date..........................19......

Robe measurement form, circa 1924. *Author's collection.*

but was likely much less than that. As other historians have noted, both the men's KKK and the women's WKKK organizations brazenly inflated their membership totals to provide the general public with an illusion of a stronger and more popular Klan.

Also indicated from this meeting, the allure of wearing the Klan's notoriously iconic white robes was waning among the membership. Excellent Commander Tess Trainer instructed, "The officers at least must wear their robes" at the meetings within the Klavern.[65] With no explanation for the deviance related to the robe-wearing, there is only speculation about whether it was due to a lack of comfort, growing feelings of social uneasiness or embarrassment or simply a backlash to the recurring monotony of Klavern rituals and obligations. Regardless of the reasoning, the discussions surrounding the wearing of robes spurred the idea that the Grey Eagles should attempt to purchase the robes of delinquent members and possibly those from families of deceased members. The two-dollar buy back amount that was agreed on was not an arbitrary price point. At the national level, the WKKK's production cost for a new robe, including the patch, facemask, waist rope and helmet, was also two dollars. The complete garment would be sold to a new member for $5.00 ($70.60 by 2018 standards). Instead of the national WKKK organization making the hefty profit off a new member's robe purchase, the Grey Eagles would be able to offer an initiate a preowned robe at a discounted rate and keep any profit generated within the coffers of the local chapter.

The meeting notes are as follows:

- *Report...Basket Social at Shaffer's...total $33.05*
- *Proceeds...building fund, ½ to the men's credit and ½ to the ladies...*
- *Hereafter, ladies to keep their ½ of the proceeds in own treasury*
- *Note of thanks...to Peterson and Shaffer for opening their homes for socials*
- *...interesting report of the Realm meeting in Milwaukee...Mrs. Goodrich was the Imperial Representative for Mrs. Robbie Gill-Comer, it was reported...28 chartered Klans in the state—each less than 100 in membership*
- *Excellent Commander has given instructions...officers must wear their robes in Klonklave...also stated that we purchase robes of delinquent members, Mr. Waller wishes to sell his wife's*
- *Motion...by Hansen, seconded by Strong..purchase robes...for $2.00...carried*

- *Excellent Commander's expenses to Milwaukee...$1.89...refunded $8.11*
- *Strong...invitation to meet (at her home) on December 14th, on account of bad roads meeting not held*
- *Constitutions sold—5—$1.25*
- *Members Present—20*
- *Tess Trainer—Excellent Commander*
- *Adella Ellsworth—Kligrapp*[66]

2

1928

Klonklave No. 11

January 18, 1928, Wednesday, 8:45 p.m.

In the New Year's Eve edition of the *Eau Claire Leader*, a front-page article offered a preview of the political war that would be waged between the KKK and American Catholics in 1928. It read, "Governor Al Smith Refuses Probe Asked by Klan." The story was in response to the New York Klan's insistence that Albany police had interfered in its 1927 Memorial Day parade.

Governor Smith, who had quickly become the most feared and despised man within Klan circles, bristled back and exclaimed, "I regard the purpose of your organization with abhorrence and I consider them subversive to the fundamentals of American democracy."[67] As Smith strategically positioned himself to become the first Roman Catholic presidential nominee of a major party in U.S. history, the Grey Eagles were eager to keep him out of the White House.

With their last three Klonklaves cancelled due to either cold weather or winter road conditions, the January 18 meeting proved that the twenty women in attendance were eager to make up for lost time. The fate of the new Klavern building fund was still far from certain, so Excellent Commander Tess Trainer was motivated to get another box social fundraiser scheduled.

Form 111

KLORAN
or
RITUAL
of
THE WOMEN
of the
KU KLUX KLAN

Nº 30317

1928

IMPERIAL HEADQUARTERS
WOMEN of the KU KLUX KLAN
LITTLE ROCK, ARKANSAS

PARKE-HARPER CO., LITTLE ROCK

The WKKK Kloran, or ritual book, circa 1928. *Author's collection.*

Klanswoman Clara Lange offered to host the event at her home, and Trainer eagerly offered her assistance.

Thirty-six-year-old Clara Lange was born Clara Helen Gamper in 1881. After marrying George A. Lange Jr. in 1917, Clara and her husband had two sons, Harlyn and Sylvin, and lived on a sprawling farm in nearby Lafayette Township. Situated near the present-day grounds of the Northern Center State Hospital, the Lange farm was midway between Chippewa Falls and Lake Wissota.[68] The Langes traveled into the city frequently because of their busy social calendars. Both were parishioners of the First Presbyterian Church and regular participants in Freemasonry, including Masonic Lodge no. 176 and the women's Order of the Eastern Star.[69] Later in life, Clara became a hosting member of the Lafayette Women's Club, an affiliate of the international General Federation of Women's Clubs. Differing greatly from political organizations like the WKKK or the Woman's Christian Temperance Union, the Federation of Women's Clubs was squarely focused on the promotion of civic and social improvements, while purposely seeking to avoid divisive issues such as prohibition, immigration, race and religion.

In 1928, however, Clara Lange was still enthralled with the WKKK. Serving as the Klavern's Klokard, or lecturer, Clara would have been charged to memorize and recite several passages found within the WKKK's Kloran, or ritual-filled handbook. During the opening ritual at each meeting, Clara would answer questions posed by the excellent commander, including "What does the flag symbolize?" and "why the fiery cross?"[70]

Clara also filled the role of Kladd, or conductor. This consisted of setting up the Klavern with the order's symbolic objects, including the Bible, water-filled container, sword, altar flag, flag on a stand and bright fiery cross lit with candles. She would also be in charge of verifying the membership of each woman present. If a member was asked, the Kladd would have the member reveal to the order's predetermined password and sign. This system of identification was common practice in several social organizations of the era, as passwords and signs prevented outside infiltrators and added a layer of mystery and secrecy to the group's ritualism.[71]

The meeting notes are as follows:

- *Due to bad roads, cold weather, and holidays…not enough to hold meeting*
- *Box social…Lange and Trainer on Kitchen Committee*
- *Current events given…*
- *Members Present—20*
- *Tess Trainer—Excellent Commander*
- *Adella Ellsworth—Kligrapp*[72]

Klonklave No. 12

February 1, 1928, Wednesday, 8:45 p.m.

Just days before a group of ten Grey Eagles braved the Wisconsin cold to join a sparsely attended winter Klonklave, the *Eau Claire Leader* featured two front-page announcements by the imperial office of the men's Klan in Atlanta, Georgia. Imperial Wizard Dr. Hiram Evans had brainstormed some ideas that he hoped would reenergize public support for the hooded order.

First, Evans threatened reprisal against any Klansman who supported Al Smith for president. Fearing that the governor was building a consensus among Democratic Party supporters across the country, Evans warned his rank and file that "any member of the organization who voted for Al Smith…would be banished from the order."[73]

In his second decree, Evans ordered the permanent removal of the face mask from the Klan's infamous triangular-shaped helmet. "Every unit of the Klan will be required to banish the mask within a month," Evans proclaimed. He explained how the rank and file members had wanted this change for quite a while because they would prefer to show their faces rather than hide behind a mask. Evans later admitted that the Klan was reacting to the rash of "anti-mask laws" that were sweeping the country as municipal, county and state governments realized that stripping the members of their public anonymity greatly reduced the group's potency within a region. The newspaper speculated that the Klan was fearful of eventual adoption of federal legislation, so they decided to "make the move first."[74]

In reality, it was the growing number of violent incidents involving mask-wearing Klansmen that caused the national organization to discard the accessory. Several psychological studies involving humans and the wearing of masks, including those done by Purdue University psychologists Franklin Miller and Kathleen Rowold, have shown how masked individuals are more likely to break social norms, as compared to their unmasked counterparts. In the case of the KKK, particularly among the men, the secrecy afforded through the mask provided a false sense of social, political and legal protection.[75] As newspapers covered horrific acts of Klan violence across the United States, Evans believed that the elimination of the mask would finally put an end to the organization's bad publicity.

In the coming days, Imperial Commander Robbie Gill-Comer would release a similar decree on behalf of the WKKK. In the meantime, the February 1 meeting of the Grey Eagles made no reference to Evans's announcements. Instead, the women reflected on the disappointing results from their most recent box social and discussed ways to increase membership participation.

To best accomplish this, the Grey Eagles decided to implement a three-pronged approach. First, members who didn't attend the box socials would be solicited for a monetary donation. Second, a Klavern bulletin would be mailed out to stimulate interest in the meetings. Finally, a roll call of the membership roster would be read at the start of each meeting. As frustrating as the attendance issue had become for the women of Klan no. 14, this particular meeting found them gathering with the men as relative coequals. They ended their meeting early and joined the "men's meeting for a program," proving just how politically potent they had become within the eyes of the men.[76]

The meeting notes are as follows:

- *Report of box social…small crowd…proceeds $6.00…games played…and a paper read…*
- *Valentine party discussed, laid over…*
- *Kligrapp suggested we have roll call in the future…adjourned to the men's meeting for a program*
- *Members Present—10*
- *Tess Trainer—Excellent Commander*
- *Adella Ellsworth—Kligrapp*[77]

Klonklave No. 13

February 15, 1928, Wednesday, 8:45 p.m.

Leading into the February 15 Klonklave, the legal saga involving men's KKK lecturer Pat Malone was back on the front page of the *Eau Claire Leader*. Malone had filed a lawsuit against Barron County Klan leader Ralph Hammond, now Grand Dragon of the entire Wisconsin Realm of the men's Ku Klux Klan, argued that the hooded order had promised to pay his $500 in legal fees from his 1927 libel case. The Wisconsin Realm of the men's KKK had no intention of paying Malone without a legal fight. Hammond's attorney submitted a demurrer, or objection to the basic legal validity of the claim, to Chippewa County Circuit Court judge James Wickham. The Klan argued that any contract that may or may not have been made was "against public policy and without consideration." In a victory for Malone and his Chippewa Falls attorney Paul H. Raihle, the judge overruled the demurrer request. Judge Wickham explained that this case "could only be decided by a trial upon its merits."[78]

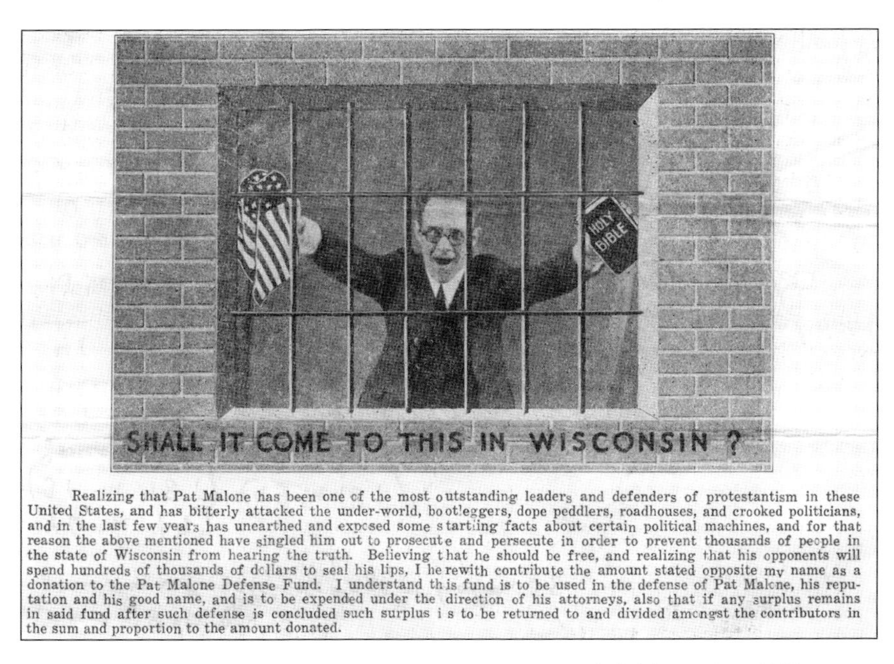

Realizing that Pat Malone has been one of the most outstanding leaders and defenders of protestantism in these United States, and has bitterly attacked the under-world, bootleggers, dope peddlers, roadhouses, and crooked politicians, and in the last few years has unearthed and exposed some startling facts about certain political machines, and for that reason the above mentioned have singled him out to prosecute and persecute in order to prevent thousands of people in the state of Wisconsin from hearing the truth. Believing that he should be free, and realizing that his opponents will spend hundreds of thousands of dollars to seal his lips, I herewith contribute the amount stated opposite my name as a donation to the Pat Malone Defense Fund. I understand this fund is to be used in the defense of Pat Malone, his reputation and his good name, and is to be expended under the direction of his attorneys, also that if any surplus remains in said fund after such defense is concluded such surplus is to be returned to and divided amongst the contributors in the sum and proportion to the amount donated.

Pat Malone's lawsuit against the men's Klan caused internal divisions, circa 1928. *Author's collection.*

As for the Grey Eagles, this meeting was their first opportunity to implement their new attendance strategies. First, they read aloud a roll call of the Klavern's members who were in "good standing" with their dues. Next, each woman in attendance was asked to share a "current event or a topic of interest" after their name was called. Although Klan secretary Adella Ellsworth did not keep a written record of what each woman shared that evening, the legal case regarding Malone and his locally hired attorney was likely a hot topic.

One of the highlights found within the meeting minutes was the women's acknowledgement of their use of secret Klan passwords. A way of identifying an officially sanctioned Klanswoman from a nonmember, passwords were also used to test the loyalty of the rank and file. If a Grey Eagle was entrusted with the secret password, would she keep it a secret? Some of these passwords, or code words, were more common than others. The code word "AYAK," which stood for "Are You a Klanswoman?" would be used in the form of a question from one member to another. The responding Klanswoman would respond, "AKIA," or "A Klanswoman I AM." Aside from providing a perception of Klavern security, the passwords made them feel that they were privileged with sensitive information that others in the community were not.

Other than the functionality and usage of secret passwords, these particular Klonklave minutes revealed the generosity and thoughtfulness that the Grey Eagles bestowed on their own struggling members. The women in attendance surprised Klanswoman Nettie Bollom while she was in the kitchen preparing the evening "lunch" by authorizing the Klavern to cover what she owed in quarterly dues. Meanwhile, the ladies discussed the preliminary stages of hosting a box social to pay off the dues owed by their ever-growing list of dues-delinquent members. The women also envisioned that if any extra money remained from that social it could be donated to needy Klan families.

Their final goodwill gesture was to buy "Sunshine," likely flowers and a get-well card, for Minnie Kurth. The thirty-two-year-old Minnie was a farmer's wife who lived with her husband, Orrin, and their three young children on a sprawling homestead in the Township of Lake Hallie.[79] From one of the most trusted and respected families in the area, Orrin also served as Lake Hallie town clerk from 1925 until 1959. Excellent Commander Tess Trainer was supportive of the get-well offering. Like Trainer and her husband, the Kurths were consistent attending members of the Christ (Episcopal) Church near downtown Chippewa Falls.[80]

Finally, the women of Klan no. 14 would soon find out whether the national Women of the Ku Klux Klan organization was going to adopt the no-mask policy decreed by the men's Imperial Wizard Dr. Hiram Evans. A "special Klonklave" was scheduled for February 22 by the national Imperial Commander herself, Mrs. Robbie Gill-Comer. The announcement that was to be read the next week was such a profound change to the operations of the order that Gill-Comer requested for all members, including those who were delinquent in their dues, to be physically present and available within their local Klaverns to hear the urgent news.[81]

Before the women closed the Klavern, they joined together in the singing of "Blest Be the Tie That Binds." Originally written by British pastor and theologian John Fawcett in 1782, this Christian hymn became a staple of Kloranic rituals within both the KKK and the WKKK.[82] Printed in the WKKK's "MusiKlan" booklet so the women could read along with the words, the song's third verse must have resonated deeply with the women that evening: "We share out mutual woes, our mutual burdens bear; and often for each other flows, the sympathizing tear."[83]

The meeting notes are as follows:

- *Roll call of members in good standing…those present responding with current event or topic…*
- *Password taken…*
- *Bollom sent to the kitchen…in her absence it was moved by Tracy, seconded by Campbell that her dues be paid…carried*
- *Box Social to be arranged to pay the dues of delinquent members… in straitened circumstances…remainder be divided between two poor families…laid over…*
- *Notice…by the Imperial Commander for February 22nd…mail out to all members…(good standing or not)*
- *Paper given by Smock on women in politics…*
- *…buy Sunshine for Mrs. Minnie Kurth (broken ankle)*
- *Closed by singing "Blest Be the Tie That Binds"…*
- *Members Present—10*
- *Tess Trainer—Excellent Commander*
- *Adella Ellsworth—Kligrapp*[84]

KLONKLAVE NO. 14 (SPECIAL)

February 22, 1928, Wednesday, 9:00 p.m.

Gathering en masse to be the first to hear the WKKK's announcement of their new no-mask decree, the Grey Eagles doubled the attendance from their previous Klonklave. Excellent Commander Tess Trainer used the event to get each woman to reaffirm her commitment to the order by strategically integrating a refresher on the "constitutional duties of each officer" and reading job descriptions and Klavern expectations aloud.

The Klan's Kludd, or chaplain, read aloud twenty-one verses from the book of Romans in the Holy Bible. As the women solemnly stood in a circle in the middle of the Klavern, they were reminded to present their bodies as a "living sacrifice" and not be "conformed to this world" but to be "transformed" by the renewing of their minds.[85] Verses three through eight reminded the Klanswomen to display a right attitude toward others, while nine through twenty-one outlined the guiding principles for leading a Christian life, including an emphasis on love, godly character, thoughtfulness and charity for one's enemies.[86] The decision to include these specific verses was not only to forge a tighter bond among those in attendance but also to prepare the women for an adversity that may arise from the impending loss of the Klan's public anonymity. Any Grey Eagle who had kept their participation a secret now ran the risk of exposure to public scrutiny, including criticism, confrontations and economic boycotts.

The text of Imperial Commander Robbie Gill-Comer's no-mask order was worded similarly to the men's decree. The excellent commander was instructed to physically remove each woman's mask from the helmet. She said that "no woman should ever wear the mask again or fraternize with a woman wearing such a mask."[87] One by one, Trainer removed each woman's mask for good. To prepare the members for this new era of transparency, Trainer had each woman "reconsecrate" their commitment

MRS. ROBBIE GILL COMER
Imperial Commander

National WKKK Imperial Commander Robbie Gill-Comer, circa 1925. *Author's collection.*

by retaking the oath of the order. The three-page Oath of Allegiance involved each member swearing to abide by an extensive list of attitudes and behaviors that were categorized into "obedience, secrecy, fidelity, and Klanishness."[88] Under the direction of the Imperial Commander, Trainer was doing everything in her power to keep the group's roster intact.

After the closing of the special Klonklave, Trainer took the unusual step of meeting with her cabinet to discuss the "urgent business" related to the new Klavern building. Since the Grey Eagles hadn't hosted a successful fundraiser in months, the women needed to get creative with their finances. To meet the deadline for a fifty-dollar payment to the men's group, they shifted money from the general fund to the building fund. In addition, they discussed the possibility of selling the group's piano to raise the additional money needed.[89]

The meeting notes are as follows:

- *…singing entire hymn "America,"…all robed*
- *…pledged allegiance to the flag…singing "Faith of Our Fathers"*
- *While standing…prayers offered…the circle, Kludd read the 12th Chapter of "Romans"*
- *Letter…from Imperial Commander…masks to be removed from all robes…no woman should ever wear the mask…or fraternize with a woman wearing…masks of those present removed…*
- *Each…asked to reconsecrate herself to the ideals of the Klan… retaking of oath…*
- *Excellent Commander called cabinet together…urgent business*
- *…money needed…to meet the taxes on the Klavern…carried*
- *…discussion as to condition and sale of piano…*
- *Members Present—19*
- *Tess Trainer—Excellent Commander*
- *Adella Ellsworth—Kligrapp*[90]

Klonklave No. 15

February 29, 1928, Wednesday, 8:30 p.m.

Following the Klan's elimination of the mask, Imperial Wizard Evans tried to shift media attention by announcing a "new degree," or level of fraternal learning, within the men's Klan. Called the Knights of the Great Forest, he advertised it as a way for existing members to expand into "new and larger activities in our national life." Evans explained that while his order had "no political ambitions," it was now prepared to promote "100 percent Americanism by stopping unrestricted immigration" into the United States. He believed that issue alone would reignite the Klan's waning popularity. With the presidential election roughly eight months away, Evans could not afford a mass exodus of members. He hoped the new degree would generate enthusiasm for the order, whether it was for current, former or aspiring members. Coincidently or not, the degree would also serve as an additional revenue stream for the cash-hungry order.[91]

The new Knights of the Great Forest degree was largely lampooned by the Wisconsin press. The *Oshkosh Northwestern* skewered the name by writing that the Klan was a "forest from the start, a dark forest of intolerance, vicious practices, and ignorance." The paper joked that the "Klan has officially realized they are lost in the woods."[92] In defense of the degree, two members of the Women's Ku Klux Klan in Oshkosh wrote a letter to the editor titled "Nice, Lady Like Order?" They argued that the reported "acts of mob violence" had "never been the policy of the KKK, nor have been officially permitted." The women added that while "all robes are accounted for," anyone with "sheets and pillow slips are always available for fake Klan raids by fake Klansmen." They concluded by comparing seekers of the "Knights of the Great Forest" degree to majestic trees reaching "maturity" that will soon "guard the gates of immigration and protect the American standard of living."[93]

As for the Grey Eagles, the turnout at the February 29 meeting was disappointing. Just seven days prior, Excellent Commander Trainer had tried to use the no-mask announcement as an opportunity to motivate the others to get more active. Regrettably for Trainer, any momentum she had created was stymied because the meeting date had fallen on a leap day. The confusion led to only eight members showing up at the meeting.

Those present did make important decisions. First, the women decided to realign their meeting schedule to the men's unit. They also decided to form their own WKKK ladies chorus, consisting of Tess Trainer, Myrtle Hansen, Nettie Bollom and Flora Campbell. The musical quartet would be accompanied by Grace Tracy as pianist and instructed by a thirty-one-year-old music teacher named Ethel Mary Tilton.

Periodically advertising herself as "Ethel Mary Tilton, Teacher of Singing," Ethel was the unmarried daughter of William and Mollie Tilton of Chippewa

Falls.[94] The Tilton family lived in a two-story home at 617 Coleman Street on the West Hill of the city of Chippewa Falls. Ethel had recently moved out of her parent's home to pursue a full-time music teaching position in nearby Eau Claire.[95] While there is no evidence that either Mollie or Ethel Tilton were dues-paying members of the Grey Eagles, family evidence suggests that they were supporters of the group. Just a year earlier, the *Chippewa Herald* reported that Ethel's father was "alleged to be a high official of the Ku Klux Klan, it being claimed that he served as Great Titan of the order for the territory surrounding Eau Claire and Chippewa Falls."[96]

Though the census reported William Tilton's occupation as "real estate," he had been arrested in February 1927, for illegally practicing medicine without a state license. Tilton had been illegally treating as many as nine hundred cancer patients with a mysterious home remedy. After he "read about cancer in different books," Tilton created what he considered a cure of "black paste" and "yellow salve" for surface tumors and a "dark medicine" for internal cancers. He boasted that only fourteen of his cancer patients had not been cured.[97] A Chippewa County jury reached a far different conclusion, as it only took fifteen minutes to reach a guilty verdict, resulting in a $500 fine and a one-year suspended sentence in state prison.[98] Later in life, William Tilton was better remembered for a twelve-acre "gravel island" he donated to the First Methodist Church's Scout Troop, called the Mollie A. Tilton Memorial Park or Scout Island.[99]

In addition to forming the choral ensemble, the Grey Eagles decided to cancel the upcoming box social due to the lack of members. Energized by the formation of their new chorus, the Grey Eagles ended the evening by voting to keep the piano for yet another season.[100]

The meeting notes are as follows:

- *…meeting not according to our constitutional date it being leap year… changing dates to correspond with men's moved by Hansen, seconded by Grace Tracy…carried*
- *…Bernice Lynn of Anson Unit…reinstated into Chippewa unit…*
- *…request from the men's orchestra that we form a ladies chorus, Ethel Tilton to be instructor…Myrtle Hansen, Nettie Bollom, Tess Trainer, Flora Campbell, and Grace Tracy as pianist*
- *…decided to keep piano for another season*
- *Members Present—8*
- *Tess Trainer—Excellent Commander*
- *Adella Ellsworth—Kligrapp*[101]

KLONKLAVE NO.16

March 14, 1928, Wednesday, 8:45 p.m.

With the scheduling conflict caused by the leap year behind them, the Grey Eagles now held their biweekly meetings on the same date as the men. The women had more than proven their ability to operate their own successful Klavern and likely viewed the change as a way to improve attendance within both Klan organizations. Husbands and wives could now consolidate their transportation to and from the Klavern, saving time and money.

During this particular meeting, the women managed both good and bad news. They exuded excitement about their newly formed choral ensemble. Originally created with four members and a pianist, both Clara Lange and Olga Smock decided to join the ranks.[102] The potential benefits of putting together a successful musical group were not lost on the ladies. Since their Klan's inception, the women had relied on internal donations from box socials and lunches to cover their Klavern's expenses. If they were going to secure long-term viability, they would need to branch out and raise money from outside the Klan.

Both national Klan organizations had success using music to enhance the popularity of their rallies, gatherings and fundraisers. Businesses like the Starr Piano Company in Indiana, which recorded a male choral ensemble called the Logansport Ku Klux Klan Quartet, produced nationally distributed records featuring songs like "Bright Fiery Cross" and "Onward Valiant Klansmen." By the time the national WKKK had formed, a similar ladies ensemble, called the Logansport Women of the Ku Klux Klan Quartette, released a phonographic record featuring the songs "Women of the Ku Klux Klan," "Here to America" and "My Old Machine."[103] Although the Grey Eagles were not expecting their choral ensemble to achieve national stardom, they certainly hoped their talents would be worthy enough to expand their upcoming fundraising opportunities.

KKK records mixed popular Christian hymns with Klan-inspired lyrics, circa 1924. *Author's collection.*

The excitement surrounding the expanded chorus was tempered with the news that the mother of Klanswoman Mary Hempelman had died. In the continued spirit of sisterhood, the Grey Eagles sent flowers to the family. Mary, who was born in Wisconsin to immigrant parents from Canada, married a Township of Lake Hallie farmer by the name of Earl Hempelman. With no children of their own, thirty-nine-year-old Mary and her husband shared residency on their farm with a laborer named John Plunkett.[104] The death of her mother would not be the only life-altering tragedy she would face. Four years later, Mary's husband, Earl, perished as a result of an accidental gun shot during a northern Wisconsin deer hunting trip.[105]

The meeting notes are as follows:

- *...progress of the Chorus...Lange and Smock added...*
- *...pay the bill of $1.50 for flowers for Hempelman's mother...*
- *Members Present—11*
- *Tess Trainer—Excellent Commander*
- *Adella Ellsworth—Kligrapp*[106]

Klonklave No. 17

March 28, 1928, Wednesday, 8:30 p.m.

With an impressive total of fourteen members in attendance, the transition to a shared meeting night continued to pay dividends. A friendly wager had been placed between the two orders to see which Klan would turn out more members for the March 28 meeting. The men's unit won, so the women had to supply a meal for everyone at the conclusion of their respective meetings.

In addition to the continued improvements made by their choral "Glee Club," the women also discussed two social issues that drew interest, including "obedience and children" and voting. A letter from the state's WKKK realm office in Milwaukee included information on both issues, including a general observation that "today's youth" didn't show the same "level of respect" to elders as past generations had. Also supplementing this claim were excerpts from the WKKK's booklet "Creed of Klanswomen," which stated, "We Believe in the American home as the foundation upon which rests secure the American Republic, the future of its institutions, and the liberties of its citizens," and "We Believe in the equality of men and women in political, religious, fraternal, civic, and social affairs wherein there should be no distinction of sex."[107]

One member who believed in the power of obedient children and female suffrage was Cora Darbe. Sharing a similar divorce history as Excellent Commander Tess Trainer, Cora had been married twice. Originally born Cora Trepus in 1871, she first married Herman Hunt at the age of twenty-three, and they had a son named Arthur. The marriage ended in legal separation, resulting in her living as a single mother for several years. Cora remarried a Chippewa Falls farmer named Edward Darbe.[108] Their union culminated in the birth of Cora's second child—a daughter named Betty. By the time she had reached the age of fifty-four, in 1928, Cora could boast of having a hardworking Methodist husband, two children of her own and a prosperous farmstead in the township of Tilden.[109]

The meeting notes are as follows:

- *Password taken...letter from State Office read*
- *Several discussions...obedience of children, voting, etc.*
- *...progress of Glee Club...contest for number in attendance...ladies were losers...had to furnish lunch*
- *Members Present—14*
- *Tess Trainer—Excellent Commander*
- *Adella Ellsworth—Kligrapp*[110]

Klonklave No. 18

April 25, 1928, Wednesday 8:30 p.m.

With the exception of the Klan's no-mask policy, newspaper coverage of the hooded-order in western Wisconsin had been sparse. By the end of April, coverage noticeably intensified. On April 1, the *Chippewa Herald*'s Voice of the People had published thoughts of a man who described himself as a "Republican all his life." Lamenting about how Wisconsin had become a "KKK State" and that the Republican Party's association with the hooded order would ruin them in the fall elections, he announced he would be willing to bet anyone $1,000 that the next president would end up being a Democrat.[111]

On the following day, both area newspapers published a bombshell confession from the former Grand Dragon of the Indiana men's Ku Klux Klan. D.C. Stephenson had been serving a life sentence for the brutal rape and murder of twenty-eight-year-old Madge Oberholtzer in 1925. He now confessed that the Indiana men's Klan had controlled several members of both the state's legislature and judges within the court system. He added that the Klan had engaged in mob violence, destroyed Catholic churches and hosted whipping parties. Stephenson added that the Indiana Klan had kept several women on the payroll whose job it was to "trap men" through the use of sex and sexual advances, as the order sought to ruin the reputations of its opponents. For the second time in three years, Stephenson delivered a devastating blow to the Klan's public image of 100 percent Americanism and law and order.[112]

The newspapers also covered a federal court case in Pennsylvania that piled on more bad news. In a countersuit filed by five former members of the men's Klan, one member from Texas claimed that Imperial Wizard Evans had personally given permission for his Klavern to burn a local white man to death. Another member from Ohio testified that his Klavern had a group called the "Night Riders" whose job was to "burn churches and to carry out bombings and assassinations." He testified that the group purposely bombed the Klan's own temple building in Dayton, Ohio, to stir up controversy and increase membership.[113]

The most startling admission from the federal case was the deposition of former Ku Klux Klan founder William J. Simmons. He testified in full support of the five former Klan members and argued that Hiram Evans had overthrown him with the help of Indiana's David Stephenson. Simmons explained that the Evans-led Klan had devolved into a "destructive" force that was "contrary to its original plan and purposes." He added that "Evans's regime is grossly disgusting, and very evidently manifests everything else but a spirit and purpose of constructive patriotism."[114]

While the national Klan managed the fallout from the blistering publicity, the Grey Eagles met only once in April. Missing from this meeting were both Tess Trainer and Kligrapp Adella Ellsworth. Both women also served as elected officers within the Chippewa Falls chapter of the Woman's Relief Corps (WRC) and were double-booked that evening for meetings. At least three other Grey Eagles, including Myra Ayers, Bernice Lekvin and Henrietta Tracy, also attended the WRC meeting in lieu of the Klan meeting.[115]

Founded in 1883, the Woman's Relief Corps was created as an auxiliary unit to the men's Grand Army of the Republic. Seeing the disastrous effects of the Civil War, the WRC formed to aid and assist the most vulnerable veterans, widows and orphans. The era predated the social welfare programs of the 1930s, so organizations like the WRC provided the most embattled, war-torn populations with much-needed economic, social and political assistance.[116]

The WRC also sought to keep the memories of fallen soldiers alive through the circulation of patriotic education in public schools and elsewhere. From both a cognitive and ideological standpoint, women like Tess Trainer would have viewed their memberships within the WRC and the WKKK as similarly aligned to their ideals of patriotism and service to country.

Despite the absence of Trainer and the other regulars, those in attendance forged ahead and made key decisions. First, the women voted to give the rights of their old piano to the men's unit. In return, the men would donate ten dollars to the Klavern's building fund in the name of the Grey Eagles and would grant the women full written permission to use the piano. The women also scheduled their next fundraising event and set a date for their glee club's first performance. With little revenue since the start of the year, the women felt pressure to generate more cash. Choral instructor Ethel Tilton hoped that the glee club could integrate a short theatrical play in the overall performance. Klanswomen Myrtle Hansen, Nettie Bollom, Tess Trainer, Flora Campbell, Clara Lange, Olga Smock and Grace Tracy, as the pianist, were tasked with honing their acting skills.

Klanswoman Olga Smock ran the meeting as smoothly as she could. Fifty-four-year-old Smock had only missed one Klan meeting since the group's inception, which made her a logical fill-in for Trainer. Her position in the Klavern was Klokan Chief, or principal advisor and investigator of candidates. Smock, like so many of the other Klanswomen, was married to a farmer and lived a few miles north of the city in the township of Tilden. Olga and her husband, Delmar, never had any children. She was an industrious woman who spent her free time being active in several social organizations.[117] She belonged to a major Wisconsin farmer's advocacy group called the Farmer's Equity Union.[118] Along with her fellow Klanswoman Ella Mason, Smock attended the meetings of a Republican Party–affiliated group called the Tilden Progressive Club.[119] Along with Klanswoman Agnes Clark, Smock was a member of the Pythian Sisters, a female auxiliary of the fraternal Knights of Pythias organization.[120] Supplementing Smock's interests in farming and politics was her strong Christian faith, as both Olga and Delmar were regular attendees at the

Several Grey Eagles were also members of the WRC, circa 1910. *Author's collection.*

Presbyterian Church in downtown Chippewa Falls. Smock certainly was a woman who had the experience, confidence and trust of the membership to facilitate a meeting in the absence of Tess Trainer.

The meeting notes are as follows:

- *…meeting by Smock*
- *Motion by Clark, seconded by Earl, to let men have piano…$10.00 to be applied on the Building Fund and give us written agreement or guarantee to have use of the new piano*
- *Supper and sale…May 18th*
- *Miss Tilton expects to put on musical…June 1st and asked the ladies to put on a little playette…*
- *Members Present—9*
- *Olga Smock—Filling-In for Excellent Commander*
- *Nettie Bollom—Kligrapp (Pro Tem)*[121]

KLONKLAVE NO. 19

May 9, 1928, Wednesday 8:30 p.m.

After appearing in the Eau Claire Leader under the Voice of the People, Imperial Wizard Evans tried to mitigate the public relations damage from the past several weeks. He lambasted the five men who testified against the Klan in court and explained that each was a known liar who had been banished from the order. Evans went on to reaffirm the virtues of the KKK as the "one agency in America fighting to protect America for Americans." He added, "It is the one agency that believes that the perpetuity of free government, liberty, and free conscience depend upon the supremacy of the Protestant faith." Noticeably, Evans avoided all of the accusations made by former Indiana Grand Dragon David C. Stephenson and former men's KKK founder William J. Simmons. He finished by painting himself as a victim, saying, "The leaders in this fight are now paying the same price that Protestant leaders have always had to pay."[122]

Back in Chippewa Falls, Tess Trainer reprised her role as excellent commander. With only seven in attendance, the meeting adjourned after just fifteen minutes. Whether the decline in attendance was related to the deeply unfavorable Klan headlines from the past month is not known. Regardless

(Bulletin:)

There will be a 35¢ plate supper, miscellaneous sale, grab-bag for the kiddies and a short program at Hallie Klavern, May 18.

Supper served at 6:30 until all are served.

E.C. (Excellent Commander)

Bulletin mailed by Excellent Commander Tess Trainer, circa 1928. *Private collection.*

of any misgivings or concerns the women may have had regarding the men's national organization, the attending women soldiered on by mailing reminders for their upcoming fundraiser. While the inside of the new tabernacle in the Township of Lake Hallie was still not finished, the outside grounds were more than sufficient for social events.[123]

The meeting notes are as follows:

- *Supper and sale…May 18th*
- *Old business…discussed*
- *Members Present—7*
- *Tess Trainer—Excellent Commander*
- *Grace Fisher—Kligrapp (Pro Tem)*[124]

Klonklave No. 20

May 23, 1928, Wednesday, 8:30 p.m.

The May 23 meeting delivered a renewed sense of normalcy, as Miss Adella Violet Ellsworth returned to her post as secretary. Originally born in Iowa in 1877, Adella was one of the few Grey Eagles who never married. At age fifty-one in 1928, she had built a noteworthy social and professional life for herself. She was an active member of the Chippewa Falls Presbyterian Church and frequently participated in its Ladies Aid and Missionary Society programs.[125] As a major proponent of education, Adella was a dedicated Sunday school teacher at the church and served as the president of children's work at the annual Chippewa County Sunday School Convention. By the early 1930s, she had earned the title of primary superintendent of the Presbyterian Church's entire Sunday School program. She maintained that position for several years.[126]

According to the 1930 federal census, Ellsworth was employed as a "practical nurse" and was listed as a "lodger" on the city's West Hill at 721 Dover Street.[127] Instead of remaining content as an occupational wage worker in the 1920s economy, Adella had visions of expanding her personal fortune through investing and speculation. The *Chippewa Herald* reported how Adella had visited Anson Township to attend a bank meeting consisting of "office holders and stockholders of the Jim Falls State Bank."[128] Like many of her fellow Grey Eagles, Adella's involvement in the WRC showed that she was also committed to helping others, including veterans and their loved ones.[129]

Adella's return to the Grey Eagles coincided with the return of several others, and attendance reached back into the double digits. This was encouraging given the battering the men's Klan had taken in the press recently. The women also regained fundraising success, as the May 18 supper and thrift sale delivered $14.94 in profit ($214.00 by 2018 standards)—the most money they had raised since January.

This meeting also reinforced how valuable the Grey Eagles had become to the success of the men's order. Instead of calling their own meeting to order, the women joined the men to hear a presentation from an unnamed national Klan speaker. One of the most prominent of the Klan's traveling political speakers was Democratic U.S. senator James Thomas Heflin from Alabama. Cotton Tom, as he was called, was a self-described white supremacist who was rumored to be a member of men's Ku Klux Klan.[130] Both the *Chippewa Herald* and *Eau Claire Leader* had republished stories that accused the senator of taking Klan money as part of a multistate speaking tour to denounce the candidacy of New York Democrat Al Smith. While it is unlikely that Senator Helfin was the guest speaker this evening, the fear of Roman Catholic Al Smith becoming president was likely the focus.

The meeting notes are as follows:

- *Meeting not called…men allowed us to attend…hear national speaker*
- *Supper and Sale, May 18th—$14.94*
- *Members Present—13*
- *Tess Trainer—Excellent Commander*
- *Adella Ellsworth—Kligrapp*[131]

Klonklave No. 21

June 6, 1928, Wednesday, 8:45 p.m.

In the two weeks leading up to the Grey Eagles' June 6 Klonklave, both the national KKK and WKKK organizations received no press coverage in area newspapers. The women's Klavern enjoyed the highest membership turnout of any meeting held so far. With twenty-three Grey Eagles in attendance, the women were in the preliminary stages of selecting officers for the upcoming year. Delivered on behalf of the nominating committee, which consisted of Klanswomen Mary Clark, Mae Connell and Anna Borgman, Chairwoman Clark released the full list of proposed officers for the attendees to consider. A forty-three-year-old wife of a farmer and dedicated mother of four children, Mary Clark took a lot of pride in the list that her committee had compiled.[132] Her second-oldest daughter, Agnes Clark, was being nominated for Klaliff, or vice-president of the Klavern. The youngest member of the Grey Eagles—only twenty-one years old—Agnes Clark was clearly seen as a rising star. Agnes was single and still eleven years away from her marriage to a farmer in the Township of Lake Hallie, so she had the time, dedication and youthful energy to shadow and learn from Excellent Commander Trainer.[133] Maybe one day Agnes would be ready to take over as leader.

Considering the elaborate rituals and memorized speaking parts that officers were expected to perform in the opening and closing of each regular Klonklave, it's conceivable that some of the women in attendance were nervous or apprehensive about being nominated and were voted into unwanted positions. For example, Clara Lange quickly refused the nominating committee's suggestion that she be elevated to Tess Trainer's position of excellent commander. With everyone else seemingly unwilling or unable to fill the role, incumbent Tess Trainer was unanimously approved to remain in her position as leader. Whether or not Trainer wanted to retain her position is not known.

The meeting notes are as follows:

- *Password taken, several letters of importance read…*
- *Bill of 30¢…envelopes and stamps…*
- *Report of Nominating Committee by Clark:*
    - *Excellent Commander—Lange*
    - *Klaliff—Kopischkie*
    - *Klokard—Connell*

  - *Kludd—Bollom*
  - *Kligrapp—Trainer*
  - *Klabee—Smock*
  - *Kladd—Borgman*
  - *Klarogo—Fisher*
  - *Klexter—Peterson*
  - *Knight Hawk—Hoover*
- *...Lange refused Excellent Commander, moved by Ellsworth, seconded by Tracy and Smock that Trainer be selected...carried*
- *Members Present—23*
- *Tess Trainer—Excellent Commander*
- *Adella Ellsworth—Kligrapp*[134]

KLONKLAVE NO. 22

June 20, 1928, Wednesday, 8:45 p.m.

With the Democratic Party's National Convention just six days away in Houston, Texas, the women of Klan no. 14 were keenly aware of its political and historical significance to the country. The Democrats were on the verge of nominating New York governor Al Smith as their choice for the presidency, and the worst fears of the Ku Klux Klan were being realized. Smith's rise was viewed as an appalling culmination of everything the Klan had warned against since its rebirth in 1915. Smith openly advertised himself as a supporter of urban immigrants, particularly those within the Irish community. Although not a first-generation immigrant himself, the sound of his New York accent over the radio seemed foreign to the ears of many rural citizens in western Wisconsin.

Smith also opposed Prohibition. Viewing the ban as an unenforceable federal overreach and a possible abuse of constitutional power, Smith angered the Klan with his support of repealing the Eighteenth Amendment. Lastly, and most significantly, Smith was a devout member of the Roman Catholic Church. The Klan organizations feared that a Smith presidency would lead to the permanent cession of United States political power to the Catholic Church's Pope Pius XI in Vatican City.[135]

The 1928 presidential election was not the first time that both Klan organizations fought to keep Al Smith out of the White House. Just four years earlier, Klan-supporting delegates at the Democratic National Convention were instrumental in preventing Smith from getting the party's nomination. The Democrats had been forced to settle on a compromise candidate—chosen on a record 103rd convention ballot—who went on to be trounced by Republican incumbent Calvin Coolidge in the general election. As both Klan organizations watched their popularity and political power wane significantly since 1924, the members of the Grey Eagles were left to wonder if it was possible to keep Smith out of the White House this time.[136]

At the June 20 meeting, the eleven women in attendance heard tantalizing details about one of the Democratic Party's delegates, a man named Mr. Petroskie. The only male Petroskie living in Wisconsin in 1928 was a Lithuanian-born immigrant who lived two hours northeast of Chippewa Falls. Whether this was the man the women were gossiping about cannot confirmed, but the presence of a recent immigrant who displayed a public penchant for political activism would have most certainly aroused the attention of the membership of Klan no. 14.[137]

In addition to the postponement of the next meeting, which inadvertently posed a scheduling conflict with the Fourth of July, Excellent Commander Tess Trainer announced a special meeting to install the new officers for the following year. She also took the liberty of appointing a handful of women to Klavern positions that didn't require the formal nomination process, as allowed by the Constitution and Laws of the Women of the Ku Klux Klan.[138]

In a sign that the future Lake Hallie Klan tabernacle was expected to be a multiuse facility that would be made available to select Protestant organizations, the minutes revealed that Klanswoman Minnie Kurth was to host her church's Ladies Aid event there. Under the invitation of a "hearty welcome to all," the Effatha Lutheran Church of Hallie advertised in the newspaper that the event would take place at the "K.K.K. Hall" on June 28.[139]

Just weeks later, the same church advertised a mission festival in the grove "near the hall," but made no mention of the name Ku Klux Klan. Whether the church faced public or private criticism for meeting at the hall is unknown, but it was the first and last time that the church advertised a public event in association with the Klan tabernacle. While the Klan's financial records indicate that Effatha was not charged a fee for using of the hall, the Grey Eagles were hoping that the new Klan Hall would generate a new and lucrative revenue stream. Unfortunately for the Klan, future meetings of the Effatha Lutheran Church were held in private homes.

As for the "challenge" issued to the Grey Eagles by the state WKKK headquarters in Milwaukee, it likely echoed the national WKKK's push for each Klavern to expand its local dues-paying membership. Events like Klanswoman Kurth's church event were likely viewed as innovative ways to recruit new members by simply opening their Klavern's doors to potentially receptive white Protestants.[140]

The meeting notes are as follows:

- *Bill...37 copies of June Bulletin—5¢ each...allowed*
- *Report...on delegate, Mr. Petroskie...National Democratic Convention...*
- *...an invitation extended...to attend any meeting of the Klan at Jim Falls*
- *A challenge from headquarters and letters from Imperial Commander and Imperial Representative read...*
- *Appointive officers by the Excellent Commander...*
    - *Klokan Chief—Clark*
    - *Klokan No. 1—Kopischkie*
    - *Kourier No. 1—Borgman*
    - *Kourier No. 2—Tracy*
    - *Music Kladd—Grace Tracy*
- *...special for July 11 to install officers, Myra Ayers installing officer*
- *Celebration for July 4th and Mrs. Kurth's Ladies Aid for June 28th, both at Klavern...*
- *Members Present—11*
- *Tess Trainer—Excellent Commander*
- *Adella Ellsworth—Kligrapp*[141]

KLONKLAVE NO. 23 (SPECIAL)

July 11, 1928, Wednesday, 8:45 p.m.

On the same day the Grey Eagles conducted their Klavern's first recorded installation of officers ceremony, the *Eau Claire Leader* published a joke regarding the nation's plummeting support for the hooded order: "The Ku Klux Klan, it is reported, is dying out. Well, there have been no lynchings for several weeks, have there?"[142]

Unbeknownst to area journalists, the July 11 meeting was an important one for the Grey Eagles of Klan no. 14. This special Klonklave held personal significance for forty-nine-year-old Myra Ayers of Chippewa Falls. Excellent Commander Tess Trainer had personally appointed the mother of two to lead the evening's installation ceremonies, which would officially swear in the officers for 1928–29. Having served as the group's Klaliff, or vice-president, for the past year, few ladies within the Grey Eagles were as well versed in the intricacies of the Klavern's rituals and ceremonies as Myra Ayers. For Commander Trainer, it was an easy decision to entrust Myra with the memory work required to correctly recite the evening's ceremony. The national WKKK's rigid protocol frowned on the members having their ritual books open during ceremonies. Not only could Myra be trusted to follow the national WKKK's installation ceremony with accuracy and precision, but all of her fellow Grey Eagles also knew that she would take personal pride in the event. On this evening, Myra Ayers would install her daughter as one of the Klavern's officers.

Born into a large southern Wisconsin farming family in 1879, Myra M. McFarlin married a rural letter carrier named Harvey Ayers in 1901.[143] After moving to Chippewa Falls in 1917, the devout Methodist couple raised two children in a comfortably modest home at 426 A Street, located across the river on the city's south side.[144] In 1928, Myra was the proud mother of a thirteen-year-old son, Stewart, and a twenty-four-year-old daughter, Bernice.[145] Myra would have the honor of swearing in her eldest child, Bernice Lekvin, to the important role of Klavern Kligrapp, or secretary.

In preparation for the installation ceremony, all members present were expected to "form in line front of the Sacred Altar facing the station of the Excellent Commander in order from left to right: Excellent Commander, Klaliff, Klokard, Kludd, Kligrapp, Klabee, Kladd, Klarogo, Klexter, Klokan, and Night-Hawk." As installing officer, Ayer's duty was to conduct the ceremony by sitting in "front of the Sacred Altar between it and the station of the Excellent Commander." Klanswoman Myrtle Hansen acted as the assistant, or Marshall, for the evening's proceedings.[146]

The following is a section of the installation:

> Marshall Myrtle Hansen: *"Almighty God, we commit to Thee these women who have been elected to fill offices of this Klan and ask that Thou wouldst fill them with wisdom and grace, that their every effort may be in tune with Thy…and this Great Order. Give them…dignity and devotion…and also teach them to be impartial in every ruling….Give them the courage to set the proper example for all Klanswomen….Oh God, we ask these things for the good of our Order and for the Glory of Thy great Name, Amen."*

Grey Eagle Myra Ayers, circa 1946. *Private collection.*

Installing Officer Myra Ayers: *"Sister Marshall, you will present the Excellent Commander for installation and read her the duties…in the Constitution of the Women of the Ku Klux Klan."*

Ceremonial Floor Procedure: *The Marshall takes the Excellent Commander by the right arm and left faces, marching to the center and in front of the Sacred Altar, turns, facing the Installing Officer. Marshall reads the charge as follows:*

Marshall Myrtle Hansen: *"The Excellent Commander is the supreme officer…she shall preside over the Klonklaves…with dignity, devotion, and impartiality…be faithful in the prompt and efficient discharge of every duty…and fearless without respect to individual persons in the administration of the affairs of her office in promoting the welfare of this Order…example to all Klanswomen of patriotism, clannishness, benevolence, love, justice, honor, and a devoted loyalty to this Order in every aspect….She shall require a faithful observance on the part of all Klanswomen within her Klanton of the Constitution, laws, usages, etc. of this Order, and all Imperial Realm or Province decrees, edicts, mandates, rulings, and instructions, and seek to make vital and effective its principles, objects, and purposes. She shall call the Klonklave to order promptly…see that her Cabinet fill their respective offices in an acceptable manner. She shall diligently safeguard the sanctity and dignity of the charter of her Klan…require the ritualistic work of the Kloran to be exemplified with the highest degree of perfection…and faithfully execute all orders and special instructions of the Realm Commander or the Imperial Commander. All communications…shall be conveyed through the Excellent Commander."*

Installing Officer Myra Ayers: *"Klanswoman Trainer, you have heard the Marshall read the duties…is it your desire that we proceed…do you accept this solemn obligation and office…?"*

Excellent Commander-Elect Tess Trainer: *"Yes."*

Installing Officer Myra Ayers: *"Sister Marshall…escort the Excellent Commander to her station."*

Ceremonial Floor Procedure: The Marshall will take the Excellent Commander by right arm, left face, and march to the station of the Excellent

> *Commander (turning to the right at corners). The Excellent Commander will remain standing, the Marshall returning to her proper place at the line of officers. The Installing Officer to take position at the left of the Excellent Commander and give two raps with the gavel which calls all Klanswomen to their feet. Then the Installing Officer says:"*
> **Installing Officer Myra Ayers**: *"Klanswomen, greet her Excellency."*
> *Ceremonial Floor Procedure: Klanswomen...give greeting (KIGY—Klanswoman I Greet You)....Excellent Commander will return the sign.... Installing Officer will seat the Klanswomen with one rap of the gavel.*[147]

One-by-one, each elected officer was read a description of their duties and asked to verbalize their understanding of them. The fifth officer in the lineup was the Kligrapp, or Klavern secretary. After the marshall concluded the reading of the secretary's constitutional duties, Myra Ayers installed her daughter.

As the marshall escorted Ayers's daughter back into the lineup, the installation carried on until all the remaining officers had been sworn in. While Myra and Bernice were not the only mother-daughter duo in Klan no. 14 (the others being Mary and Agnes Clark), they represented the highest ranking. Even though Myra had not been elected to any leadership position for the upcoming year, Bernice was poised to become the most significant member after the excellent commander. As the third-youngest member of the Grey Eagles, twenty-four-year-old Bernice had big shoes to fill, as she was set to replace the steady and experienced hand of Adella Ellsworth.

While the July 11 installation ceremony was one of the most significant moments in the young Klavern's history, an even more prestigious event took place at the Lake Hallie Klan tabernacle two weeks later. The Grey Eagles were set to host a WKKK Provincial Klonverse, or convention, for the Realm of the State of Wisconsin, and they were eager to show off their finely tuned ritual skills in their brand-new building.

The meeting notes are as follows:

- *Installation of officers...Ayers assisted by Hansen...*
- *Announcement of Mission Festival...July 22nd at the Klavern*
- *Members Present—12*
- *Tess Trainer—Excellent Commander*
- *Bernice Lekvin—Kligrapp*[148]

KLONKLAVE NO. 24 /

July 18, 1928, Wednesday, 8:45 p.m.

One week after the installation ceremony, eight of the sixteen incoming officer positions had yet to be installed. By this evening's end, only the positions of Klexter (Ruth Peterson) and Music Kladd (Grace Tracy) remained vacant. This meeting was advertised as the allotted preparation time for the following week's WKKK Provincial Convention for Province no. 2 of the Realm of the State of Wisconsin, so the Grey Eagles had much to discuss.

First, Excellent Commander Tess Trainer needed the entire membership to be well versed on the specific issues the district and state leaders would discuss at the provincial gathering. Several editions of the *Fellowship Forum* newspaper were made available for the women to read. The Fellowship Forum was the same anti–Roman Catholic organization to whom the Grey

Chippewa Falls, Wisc.
July 16 - 1928.

TO ALL KLANSWOMEN:--

This is to notify you of a BIG meeting to form Province No. 2 of the north half of the State and asking that if you are not paid up, will you do this so you may be able to attend this meeting which begins at 12:30 Wed. July 25, and a joint meeting of Klanswomen and Klansmen in the evening. You will present your dues cards at the door and bring your robes, please. If you are an officer, to be installed yet, be sure to come tihs coming Wed. night, July 18, to finish this work and get the new password and card which shall entitle you to come to the meeting July 25.

At the BIGmeet ing a registration fee of 25¢ will be charged t o cover expense of meet ing. If you are interested in the work oof our organization, I know I can count on you being there where we will be able to hear all about it and there-by better able to do our bit. It would give me great pleasure to see you there and know you are one I could depend upon, as well as our unit. You can help us, and we need you, will you be there?

In the Sacred Unfailing Bond,

E.C.

Letter sent by Tess Trainer promoting the Province no. 2 meeting in Lake Hallie, circa 1928. *Private collection.*

Eagles had donated seven dollars to jumpstart a radio station in August 1927. One of the editions included a call to arms to pass the Robsion-Capper Free Public School Bill, which sought to create a national Department of Public Education to "guarantee unto every child in America, regardless of race, creed, or color, at least a Grammar School Education."[149] This bill represented one of the few examples where the Ku Klux Klan and African American organizations found themselves in agreement. While African Americans viewed this bill as an opportunity to improve educational quality and access to black children across the country, the Klan saw the strengthening of public schools as a way to undermine parochial education.[150] To what extent the women of Klan no. 14 discussed this paradox is not known, but this particular edition of the *Fellowship Forum* illustrated how powerful and potent the Klan women were viewed by a far-right national publication.

A second point of discussion addressed by Commander Trainer was the amenities that would need to be supplied for the convention, including food, refreshments, transportation and lodging. Unfortunately, the exact itinerary for the event remains unknown. A document from the WKKK's Wisconsin Realm headquarters in Milwaukee lists the thirty-four counties that would be eligible to send representatives to the Lake Hallie Klavern in a week's time.[151]

The women of Klan no. 14 had been invited to attend a special meeting thirteen miles north of the city at the Old Anson Methodist Church near Jim Falls. While Anson Township did have a Ku Klux Klan, records of its specific activity and membership have yet to be uncovered.

The meeting notes are as follows:

- *Installation…*
  - *Klaliff—Agnes Clark*
  - *Kladd—Clara Lange*
  - *Klokard—Mae Connell*
  - *Night Hawk—Emma Hoover*
  - *Kourier (No. 1)—Anna Bergman*
  - *Kourier (No. 2)—Henrietta Tracy*
- *Several Fellowship Forums…two articles were read, "Someone ought to tell the truth about the political situation" (Lange) and "Patriotism" (Trainer)*
- *Communications from realm office read pertaining to meeting held Wed. July 25…Hansen named to look after lodging for those who had to stay, transportation to same, and get information about busses*

and trains...noon lunch to be served, 35¢ supper, and a lunch of ice cream and cake after the evening session

- *Invitation...special meeting at Old Anson Church*
- *Bill...July bulletins...*
- *Members Present—16*
- *Tess Trainer—Excellent Commander*
- *Bernice Lekvin—Kligrapp*[152]

KLONKLAVE NO. 25 (SPECIAL KLONVERSE OF PROVINCE NO. 2)

July 25, 1928, Wednesday, Time Unknown

The special convention, or Klonverse, of Province no. 2 of the Wisconsin Realm of the Women's Ku Klux Klan was arguably the most compelling event to be hosted by the Grey Eagles of Chippewa Falls in 1928. Although the total number of Klanswomen in attendance is not documented, at least thirty from the western side of the state were in attendance. Arriving by either bus, train or automobile, the delegates came from as far north as Superior, as far west as Ellsworth and as far south as La Crosse. Although the Realm of Wisconsin's Province no. 2 map technically included thirty-four western Wisconsin counties, the minutes document women from only a handful of counties, including Chippewa, Pierce, Douglas, La Crosse and Eau Claire. It is possible that additional women were in attendance who were simply not mentioned by name or geographical origins. Another potential conclusion is that by 1928 the official dues-paying membership of the WKKK in western Wisconsin had been reduced to just a handful of counties.

Despite the lingering questions surrounding the WKKK's overall membership strength within Province no. 2, the members attending the Lake Hallie Klavern were able to meet and mingle with an influential figure within Klan circles. Visiting Klanswoman Mary J. Bishop of Grand Rapids, Michigan, was a prominent and well-traveled representative for the national WKKK. Bishop had been one of the early proponents of the women's hooded order coming into the Wolverine State, and she first recruited female Michiganders shortly after the national WKKK was formed.[153] Aside from being the official head of the Realm of Michigan, Bishop also maintained the title of imperial representative for the national WKKK. As a result of her dual role, Bishop spent a substantial amount of time traveling the Midwest on behalf of Imperial Commander Robbie Gill-Comer. Because of Bishop's history as a grassroots organizer in Michigan, the national WKKK believed that she had an innate ability to connect with midwestern women and could grow operations in states where chartered Klaverns had arrived much later than others, particularly in Wisconsin.

Even though hosting a powerful woman like Bishop represented a major milestone for the Grey Eagles, neither the *Chippewa Herald* nor the *Eau Claire Leader* made any mention of the convention or Bishop. About a month later, however, the *Eau Claire Leader* published a story about Bishop and Imperial Wizard Hiram Evans leading a rally of "5,000 white robed knights" in Michigan's Upper Peninsula, which directly borders Wisconsin's northeast boundary.[154] Considering that both the KKK and WKKK were masters at drumming up local press coverage, it's likely that Bishop did not want her presence publicly advertised during the provincial convention. Due to the importance and sensitivity of what was being discussed by the women inside the Klavern, it makes sense that the women wanted to keep this particular gathering a secret.

In addition to discussing membership items and fundraising ideas, the most consequential theme to arise out of the provincial convention was the need to defeat Democratic presidential nominee Al Smith in the fast-approaching November election. Of the ten resolutions agreed on at the gathering, two were directly tied to Smith. The text of the second resolution was to "give steadfast support to…the 18th Amendment." This resolution was eventually connected to the fifth on their list, which reflected the women's deeply held convictions against the Roman Catholic governor from New York. It stated: "Resolved that we…prevent the election of a Tammanyite, a nullificationist, a dripping wet Romanist, to the Presidency of the United States."

Considering the passionate disdain for Smith's candidacy, his name was never directly mentioned within the resolution itself. As a rising star in New York City politics, Smith was certainly indebted to the party bosses of the city's Tammany Hall political machine. Both as a member of the state legislature and as governor, Smith was mindful of the political forces that mobilized the vote on his behalf. Unlike many other politicians, however, Smith was an agile and talented politician who avoided the corruption that Tammany often demanded of its members. Because Smith was the first Roman Catholic nominated by a major party, and because he was a fervent opponent of the Eighteenth Amendment, the Klanswomen forged a deeply distorted version of Smith's life and career.[155]

From the rest of the meeting's resolutions and points of discussion, it is revealed that the wearing of robes had become increasingly inconsistent in the state's Klaverns, much to the dismay of the female leaders in attendance. Whether the typical Klanswomen were not wearing their robes out of convenience, the drudgery of ritual or a growing sense of embarrassment or shame, the delegates at the provincial convention displayed no sympathy. They made a point of reiterating that every Klavern needed to improve the consistency of required uniform and regalia.

Realm Commander Mary J. Bishop of the Wisconsin WKKK, circa 1925. *Author's collection.*

As for the all-important fundraising efforts to keep each Klavern financially solvent, it was made clear in resolution number eight that the women's fundraisers should not get too socially controversial. "Dancing or card playing parties" were not allowed to be hosted under the name of the WKKK.

Lastly, the provincial convention reflected on just how respected Excellent Commander Tess Trainer had become within the larger statewide WKKK network. Trainer had been appointed by Bishop to serve as a vice-president of the Realm's state convention, or Great Klaliff.[156]

The meeting notes are as follows:

- *Meeting of Province No. 2, July 25, 1928…Lake Hallie Klavern…*
- *Mrs. Bishop…urging everyone to…prevent Al Smith's election…very necessary to wear robes at meetings…Florida was the only state in the Union whose (party convention) delegates stood 100% against Smith*
- *…Drafting Committee of 10 resolutions…given by Resolutions Committee…*
    - *No. 1 = …send wire to Imperial Commander Robbie Gill-Comer for her writing efforts on our behalf…adopted*
    - *No. 2 = …steadfast support to the Constitution of the United States, especially the 18th Amendment…adopted*
    - *No. 3 = …every paid up Klanswoman receive a Badger Bulletin…approved*
    - *No. 4 = …to Klanswomen of Chippewa Falls, we extend thanks and appreciation for courtesy and hospitality…adopted*

   - *No. 5 = …we work to prevent the election of a Tammanyite, a nullificationist, a dripping wet Romanist, to the Presidency of the United States…adopted*
   - *No. 6 = …Province No. 2, provide funds for distribution of special literature for the next (6) months…adopted*
   - *No. 7 = …every member own a robe* [sic] *and wear them to every meeting and anyone who has none to get one…adopted*
   - *No. 8 = …we as a women's organization, does not* [sic] *sponsor dancing or card playing parties…adopted*
   - *No. 9 = …we encourage attending church every Sunday, and attend some church as a body once a month…adopted*
   - *No. 10 = …we extend our love and esteem to Mrs. Bishop… adopted*
- *Five Excellent Commanders, ten chartered Klan delegates, four provisional delegates, and twenty-seven visitors registered.*
- *Klanswomen Present—46*
- *Tess Trainer—Excellent Commander*
- *Grace Fisher—Kligrapp (Pro Tem)*[157]

Klonklave No. 26

August 15, 1928, Wednesday, 8:40 p.m.

By all accounts, the Provincial no. 2 meeting of the WKKK had been a success. With their Lake Hallie Klan tabernacle on full display and nearly open for business, Trainer and her Grey Eagles had shown the other Wisconsin women that they were deeply committed to the organization and firmly dedicated to defeating Klan nemesis Al Smith in November. But it wasn't just the Grey Eagles who had been making a name for themselves in western Wisconsin. Just twenty-nine miles west, in the city of Menomonie, another ambitious chapter was making a name for itself.

On Sunday, July 29, the Menomonie area Ku Klux Klan held an enormous grand opening event for its new Klavern and tabernacle, which had been constructed north of the city limits in between North Menomonie and Menomonie Junction. Similar to the Chippewa Falls Klans, the men and women of the Menomonie Klans were eager to open a tabernacle away from downtown. Several reasons likely explain this transition, including the additional privacy and a growing desire to segregate themselves from Catholics. On a more political front, the Klan members probably preferred the jurisdiction of an elected county sheriff's department over that of a hired city police chief. Neither of the Klans were willing to completely trade convenient access to their Klaverns for advantages in other areas. Just as the Grey Eagles Klavern had been constructed two blocks off U.S. Highway 53 between Chippewa Falls and Eau Claire, the Menomonie Klan built its new headquarters just off Wisconsin State Highway 25.

Unlike the Grey Eagles, whose meetings never seemed to be covered by the Chippewa Falls or Eau Claire press, the opening of the Menomonie Klan's building was treated as front-page news. The *Eau Claire Leader* reported that roughly one thousand women and children attended the opening of the new headquarters. Likely due to the shared-use expectations for the building, the construction of the Menomonie Klavern was formalized by a group called the Dunn County Order of Protestants (DCOP). The article in the *Leader* mentioned that the building was being turned over to the Klan so that it could begin its membership drive starting on August 12. The DCOP, which had been officially incorporated by the State of Wisconsin in 1926, sold shares of common stock as an ingenious way of raising funds to cover its operating expenses. The event was celebrated with food, speeches and joyous Protestant fellowship. After a Lutheran minister gave a sermon to the girls and women in attendance, the controversial Pat Malone, who had recently returned to the area as a Klan organizer, gave one of his rousing and accusatory speeches against Catholicism.[158]

What the *Eau Claire Leader* failed to realize was that this event was celebrating much more than a new Klan tabernacle. The day's festivities were also designed to celebrate the official chartering of the Women's Ku Klux Klan in Menomonie. Named the Krimson Kross Klan, the women of Menomonie had submitted the necessary documentation to become the WKKK's thirty-second Klan unit in the state, under the leadership of their newly elected excellent commander Lenora Crosby.

Although the festivities in Menomonie had been attended by many Klansmen and Klanswomen from around Wisconsin, the Grey Eagles of Chippewa Falls made no mention of the event in their minutes. Considering the volume of Klan members who attended the initiation, it is probable to suggest that at least some of the Chippewa Falls women were present to celebrate with their new Krimson Kross sisters.

As for the Grey Eagles, the August 15 meeting revealed that the WKKK's state convention, or Klorero, would take place on the eastern

The former tabernacle of the Menomonie Klans at 2238 Wilson Street. *Photo by John Kinville.*

side of the state, in Oshkosh. Excellent Commander Tess Trainer would attend the as both a delegate and as an appointed vice-president of the entire convention. Considering the prestige and significance of Trainer's participation, the women of Klan no. 14 authorized their excellent commander to have $10 from the club's treasury to pay for unspecified expenses ($143 by 2018 standards).

In an addition to the ice cream social hosted at the home of Klanswoman Myrtle Hansen, it is revealed that the women needed to pay an interest payment to Fred Dittmar, the husband of fellow Grey Eagle Emma Dittmar. Even though the Klan's financial records show no record of this particular expenditure, it suggests that the Lake Hallie Klan Hall's ongoing construction costs may have been partially financed by the Dittmars. Regardless of the specifics of the financial arrangement, the interest payment to Fred Dittmar was a significant sum of money, $715 by 2018 standards.

The meeting notes are as follows:

- *…read communications from Imperial Representative*
- *Talked about Klorero to be held at Oshkosh, Wisconsin, September 7–8th…allow Kleeper, Tess Trainer, $10.00 for her expenses…*

- *Motion by Fisher, seconded by Clark...pay Fred Dittmar $50.00... carried*
- *...ice-cream social to be held at Bill Hansen's, Friday night, August 17th*
- *Members Present—8*
- *Tess Trainer—Excellent Commander*
- *Grace Fisher—Kligrapp (Pro Tem)*[159]

KLONKLAVE NO. 27

August 29, 1928, Wednesday, 8:30 p.m.

More than a month and half after the Grey Eagles conducted their installation ceremony, the position of musiklad, or Klavern musical conductor, had yet to be filled. For reasons not provided in the minutes, Grace Tracy was unable to fill the appointed position. As a result, Trainer turned to Lillie Clem. Her primary role would be to play the Klavern's piano during the musical numbers, such as the singing of "America." While it's possible that this was an accidental omission by the temporary secretaries who filled in for Bernice Lekvin, it's also conceivable that the members only sang musical numbers when their piano-playing musiklad was in attendance.

Klanswoman Lillie Clem, who was born Lillie F. Copper in 1887, had moved to Wisconsin from Illinois after marrying Alvertise Clem. While Alvertise worked as a train car inspector for the Soo Line Railroad in Chippewa Falls, Lillie stayed at home and raised their daughter, Grace, in their middle-class home at 828 West Elm Street.

Like many other Grey Eagles, Lillie's activities in the local WKKK represented only a fraction of her social and political connections in the community. She was active in 4-H, the Royal Neighbors of America and the Woman's Christian Temperance Union (WCTU).[160] Lillie also hosted several Ladies Aid gatherings for the city's Church of Christ, sewing parties for the American Red Cross and a plethora of social gatherings for the Christian Gospel Chapel's Young People's Society. In 1944, upon news of her untimely death at the age of fifty-seven, her WCTU sisters published an announcement in the local newspaper that all members were "requested to attend" Lillie's funeral, and they should remember to wear their WCTU bows.[161]

With the musiklad position filled, the women of Klan no. 14 began to prepare for their big fall fundraiser. In this meeting, the women decided to merge several fundraisers into one event, which would consist of a rabbit supper and a thrift sale. Last year's event netted the Grey Eagles $48.04 ($678.00 converted into 2018 dollars). As it was the only major fundraiser scheduled for the fall season, the women were keenly aware that it needed to be lucrative enough to generate the revenue required to sustain the future Lake Hallie Klan Hall's expenses.

One of the strategies that the national Women of the Ku Klux Klan had for deepening the loyalty of the existing members while generating additional revenue was the creation of auxiliary Klan units for children. At this week's meeting, Tess Trainer discussed the details of the WKKK's membership programs for children, which included the Tri-K-Klub, Junior Preparatory and Kradle Roll.

The Tri-K-Klub had been established to groom girls aged thirteen to seventeen into the world of the WKKK. Like the adult ladies' organization, the Tri-K-Klub had its own robes and regalia, rules and rituals and hierarchy of officers with designated duties. The Tri-K-Klub was viewed within Klan circles as a vital way to recruit and raise the next generation of Klanswoman into model women and future housewives while expanding Klannishness deeper in the home environment. In a letter sent by Wisconsin Realm commander Edith M. Hunt, the expansion of the Tri-K-Klub program was essential to ensuring that Protestantism would "live through the ages" and that the "most enduring education that one can be had [*sic*] is that education which is received in the tender years of one's life." The realm commander predicted that those Klantons who fully implemented the Tri-K-Klub program would see a renewed commitment from their adult female members, as they would become "more interested in their own work" while they guided their daughters through the process.[162]

As author Kathleen Blee pointed out in her book *Women of the Klan*, the expansion of the Tri-K-Klubs naturally increased revenue for the overall WKKK.[163] What is revealed within the Wisconsin Realm commander's letter, however, is that 80 percent of a teenager's membership dues would serve to benefit just three individuals within the order. Each one of these "supervisors" would receive a lucrative per-member payment for their work and organizational efforts. In her letter to all of the Klantons, Wisconsin Realm commander Hunt shared the itemized summary of how each annual $2.50 Tri-K-Klub dues membership would be allocated:

$0.50—National Supervisor, Irene Barton
$0.50—State Supervisor
$1.00—Field Supervisor
$0.50—Local Tri-K-Klub Treasury[164]

The payment allocation was a clear message that the WKKK had created a system where eager and persuasive supervisors could profit handsomely by discovering and grooming the WKKK's membership pipeline of the future. Once a Tri-K-Klub girl turned eighteen, however, she would be expected to pay an addition $2.50 to match the $5.00 membership dues of a typical adult female member, thus redirecting the profits away from the field supervisors. According to Wisconsin Realm commander Hunt, the proceeds from the additional $2.50 would be distributed based on the WKKK's standard Klectoken formula.

In addition to the Tri-K-Klub for teenage girls, the WKKK also created an auxiliary called the Junior Preparatory Department, or Junior Preps. Designed as a coeducational unit of girls and boys, the Junior Preps group was for children aged six through twelve. Wisconsin Realm commander Hunt referred to the Junior Preps as the "most valuable asset of the Women of the Ku Klux Klan." She explained, "If a child is trained during its early years such training will be lasting and these children will be anchored to the philosophies taught them...in such a way they cannot be shaken from them."[165]

Tri-K Kreed

WE, the members of the Tri--K--Klub, humbly acknowledge the supremacy of Almighty God, and the Divinity of His Son, Jesus Christ, our Lord.

Believing that the United States of America was established by the will of the Creator, and that it has been preserved under His guiding hand to serve a lofty purpose in His universal plan, we shall ever be devoted to those principles under which our government was constituted: Political liberty, religious freedom and brotherly love.

We believe we may best accomplish the noble and patriotic aims of this Klub by uniting ourselves together, a great army of komrades, seeking the knowledge and practicing the devotion which will make us real citizens of America, worthy to cherish and perpetuate our American heritage.

"DEUS, PATRIA, SOROR"

(Our God, Our Country, Our Sister)

Tri-K Klub's Kreed, circa 1928. *Author's collection.*

A final youth organization discussed by Commander Trainer and the Grey Eagles was the WKKK's Kradle Roll Department. Specifically created for all children starting at birth, a Klanswoman could register her daughter or son with their state's realm office and receive an armband for her child to wear at no cost. Each Klanswoman could then submit a photograph of her child to the state realm, where it would be added to the Kradle Roll Chart. According to Hunt, "These charts are furnished from these headquarters at a nominal cost."[166]

Even though several Grey Eagles did indeed have children eligible for all three auxiliary programs, there is no evidence that either had been officially pursued, organized or chartered. While the women of Klan no. 14 would have likely recognized and accepted the benefits of such programs, any additional membership costs would have likely dissuaded them from moving forward. It's conceivable that the women already had their children play an unofficial role within the unit, such as assisting with chores while hosting fundraising activities. In any event, no evidence from the minutes suggests that any of the members' children played a direct role in the inner workings of the Chippewa Falls WKKK.

The meeting notes are as follows:

- *Motion by Bollom, seconded by Hempelman…annual rabbit supper in connection with Harvest Festival and sale…carried*
- *Mrs. Clem…Musiklad*
- *Excellent Commander…talk on Junior Preparatory and Kradle Roll*
- *Communications from Imperial Representative M. J. Bishop*
- *Members Present—9*
- *Tess Trainer—Excellent Commander*
- *Agnes Clark—Kligrapp (Pro Tem)*[167]

Klonklave No. 28

September 19, 1928, Wednesday 8:45 p.m.

For reasons not detailed within the minutes, the Grey Eagles met only once during the month of September. Prior to this regularly scheduled September 19 Klonklave, however, there were three notable developments.

The first took place fifteen days earlier, on September 4, when a letter printed on official WKKK Imperial Headquarters letterhead was mailed to Klanswoman Bernice Lekvin, the Kligrapp of Klan no. 14. According to the letter, which was signed "Bond Department," the national office instructed the women to do the following:

> *Under provision of our Constitution…KLIGRAPPS and KLABEES are required to make bond, therefore we are today placing you…under bond. Bond premiums are based…on all sums of $1,000.00 and over the rate is twenty-five cents per hundred, or $2.50 per $1,000.00. Attached is the statement for bond premiums…should be paid out of the Klan Treasury, we will appreciate your check at your earliest convenience.*[168]

According to the Constitution and Laws of the Women of the Ku Klux Klan, the Imperial Commander had unlimited discretion as to the "manner and in such amounts" bond payments would be used. All WKKK chartered Klaverns, presumably across the country, were instructed to submit a payment based on the status of their financial holdings within their individual treasuries. Because the national WKKK believed that the Grey Eagles had more than $1,000.00 in their treasury, the total bond fee charged to the Klavern would be $5.00, or $2.50 each for the Kligrapp (secretary) and Klabee (treasurer). The reasoning behind the implementation of the bond request was not revealed in the letter.

By 2018 standards, the $1,000 in Klavern treasury holdings would be roughly $14,300. This assessment is in stark contrast with the Klabee's official report in the minutes, which divulged that the group only had $24 on hand ($343.00 by 2018 standards). It's conceivable that Imperial Headquarters had a much broader definition of what was included in the tabulation of a Klavern's treasury, especially if they considered the valuation of a partial ownership in a Klavern building. Regardless of the discrepancies, Lekvin marked the $5 fee "Paid on September 21, 1928." With just $24 in actual cash in the treasury, the Grey Eagles were not as financially solvent as Imperial Headquarters imagined them to be.

The second notable event that took place in early September was the WKKK Realm of Wisconsin State Klorero, or state convention. Unfortunately, the minutes do not reveal any specific information that Commander Trainer learned from her time at the convention. What is clear is that the women who attended the Klorero wanted to keep the gathering at least semisecret from the press. The city's newspaper, the *Oshkosh Northwestern*, made no direct mention of any WKKK-related activity in the area over September 7 and 8. Curiously, an announcement buried on page eight of the September 8 edition was an unassuming headline titled "Form Organization." The blurb explained how sixty women from around the state had gathered at Oshkosh's Hotel Raulf to create a new society. Calling themselves the "Anthar Club," which is eerily similar to the Ku Klux Klan's motto of *Non Silba Sed Anthar*, meaning "not for one's self but for others," the women attending stated that they were organized around "social and civic lines." If the name of the newly formed organization wasn't coincidental enough, one of the officers elected at the gathering of this new "Anthar Club" was none other than Tess Trainer of Chippewa Falls.

The final notable event of the month was the return of Imperial Representative and leader of the Realm of Michigan Mary J. Bishop. While attending a Klan Klonklave in the city of Cornell, twenty-four miles north of Chippewa Falls, Bishop had discussed how the women could expand their fundraising efforts. Of more pressing significance, with the presidential election less than two months away, Bishop announced the existence of the WKKK's "State Propaganda Fund" and encouraged all members to contribute. Possibly as a result, a chicken dinner fundraiser was added to the Grey Eagles' calendar for September 28.

The meeting notes are as follows:

- *Report…by Bollom…*
    - *Balance - $60.00. Half…goes to the men*
- *Robbie Gill Comer…in regards to bonding…the amount being $2.50 each…*
- *Excellent Commander…report on Klorero at Oshkosh…*
- *Mrs. Bishop at Cornell… supporting State Propaganda Fund, money raising means, etc.*
- *Chicken Supper—September 28th*
- *Members Present—12*
- *Tess Trainer—Excellent Commander*
- *Nettie Bollom—Kligrapp (Pro Tem)*[169]

Klonklave No. 29

October 3, 1928, Wednesday, 8:45 p.m.

On October 1, 1928, controversial Klan lecturer Pat Malone once again stood before the seven justices of the Wisconsin State Supreme Court. Malone was now arguing his case that the Grand Dragon of the men's Ku Klux Klan, Ralph Hammond, owed him $500 in unpaid legal aid from his successfully argued libel case.[170] Eleven days later, the *Chippewa Herald* reported that Malone's attorney had returned from Madison, "where he argued the case of Pat Malone against the Ku Klux Klan and won." For the second time in less than two years, the tempestuous Malone would leave the East Wing of the Wisconsin State Capitol victorious.[171]

In addition to the Malone case, a scathing anti-Klan letter to the editor had been published in the *Eau Claire Leader*. Written by an anonymous Catholic from Eleva, Wisconsin, the letter opened wondering "how so many could be fooled into joining an organization that was un-American in principle and unfair in its tactics." The writer bluntly asked, "How can our neighbors attend meetings where the Catholic Church is vilified…and still pretend to be our friends? The author then complained about the "whispering campaign" that members of the Klan had been engaging in to defeat the candidates they opposed for political office.[172]

With the 1928 presidential election just more than a month away, the extremely low attendance at the October 3 Klonklave must have come as a shock to Excellent Commander Trainer. After attending the State Klorero, Trainer would have been as motivated as ever to prevent Al Smith from becoming the first elected Catholic president in U.S. history. With only seven Grey Eagles in attendance, one can only wonder if Trainer had become worried about the resolve of her fellow Klanswomen leading up to the election.

In response to the Imperial Representative's call to support the WKKK's State Propaganda Fund, and likely out of concern that the Klan's message was not getting out as extensively as they had hoped, the Grey Eagles voted to send $10 ($143 by 2018 standards) to help sustain the State Realm's propaganda efforts. Unfortunately, the minutes provide no clue about what these efforts included.

Even if the lack of attendance raised concerns among the women, the results of the hastily scheduled chicken dinner delivered much-needed reassurance. Klan No. 14 netted a respectable $57.65 ($819.00 by 2018 standards).

The meeting notes are as follows:

- *…Chicken Supper—$57.65*
- *…motion by Bollom, seconded by Fisher…send $10.00 to State Propaganda Fund, carried*
- *Members Present—7*
- *Tess Trainer—Excellent Commander*
- *Nettie Bollom—Kligrapp (Pro Tem)*[173]

Klonklave No. 30

October 17, 1928, Wednesday, 9:10 p.m.

With just one week before the presidential election, Al Smith blasted the Ku Klux Klan in an address in Baltimore. He accused the Klan of being "out of line with American traditions and history" and added that he would rather go down in "ignominious defeat" than to be raised to the presidency by a gift of the people because of the influence of the Klan's "perverted ideas of Americanism." Not only did Smith argue that he didn't want Catholics to vote for him simply because he was of their same faith, but also that he didn't want people to vote for him because they felt sorry for him as a result of the Klan's vitriol.[174]

Meanwhile, the national men's Ku Klux Klan received a slew of embarrassing press coverage regarding its financial status. On October 16, the *Eau Claire Leader* published a story titled "Receivership Requested of Ku Klux Klan." A former member had filed a lawsuit claiming that Imperial Wizard Evans had rendered the group insolvent by spending excessively to wage a political campaign of "libel and slander" against Al Smith.[175] It was alleged that the men's Klan had violated the state's campaign finance laws, which banned the practice of club officers from using funds to "directly,

Al Smith in Milwaukee, Wisconsin, circa 1928. *Author's collection.*

or indirectly" influence an election or primary. If the men's KKK was indeed broke, which the order emphatically denied, the development would be extraordinary, considering it had allegedly brought in more than $100 million from its dues-paying members.[176] As the *Eau Claire Leader* newspaper joked, "Imperial Hiram Wizard Evans insists the Klan is solvent. He ought to know for he has the koin."[177]

As for the Grey Eagles, the low attendance at the final Klonklave before the election was alarming. Even the minutes themselves, which were completely devoid of any supplemental details, were bare-bones. Considering the tectonic political and cultural implications of the election, the seven in attendance were likely stunned, if not agitated, by the lack of participation by their fellow members.

As for the die-hards who did show up—Trainer, Mae Connell, Nettie Bollom, Olga Smock, Mary Clark, Emma Hoover and Grace Fisher—the next few weeks would likely be an excruciating wait. Reading the daily *Chippewa Herald* would only exasperate the anxiety because of front-page headlines like "Vigorous Campaign Nearing Close," "Chiefs of Both Parties Insist They Will Win," "Forecast Record Vote All over State" and "Extra Supply of Ballots Ready at Local Polls." With the prospect of large numbers of exuberant Catholic voters supporting Al Smith in cities like Chippewa Falls, the Women of the Ku Klux Klan needed to energize and turn out as many women as they could to stop him.

Meanwhile, the Klan had received a startling national headline just days before the vote. A Pennsylvania real estate broker had been found gagged, bound, branded and bleeding in the Bronx in New York City. Found carved into his chest were the letters KKK and found stuffed in his mouth was a pamphlet linking Al Smith to anti-Catholic sentiments.[178] As the presidential election was drawing near, national tensions were running high.

The meeting notes are as follows:

- *Correspondence read…*
- *Current events…*
- *Members Present—7*
- *Tess Trainer—Excellent Commander*
- *Grace Fisher—Kligrapp (Pro Tem)*[179]

Klonklave No. 31

November 7, 1928, Wednesday, 8:50 p.m.

A day after the election, the eleven Grey Eagles in attendance for the Wednesday Klonklave were likely savoring the national news. Al Smith had not only lost the to the Quaker Herbert Hoover but was also steamrolled electorally. Front-page headlines like the *Eau Claire Leader*'s "Landslide Carries Hoover to Victory" and the *Chippewa Herald*'s "Hoover Landslide Grows" almost certainly left the Klanswomen feeling a deep sense of accomplishment and pride. For years, the national WKKK had made Catholicism a central target in their rise to power and a rallying cry to energize and motivate women from the white Protestant fringe of the conservative end of the political spectrum. From a women's empowerment standpoint, the WKKK had consistently reminded its members that groups of organized voting women could change the cultural and political landscape of the world and the framework of the municipalities in which they resided. All they had to do, from the WKKK perspective, was work collectively, vote united and stay committed.

Carrying forty of the forty-eight states in the electoral college, Hoover had support in nearly every region of the country. Hoover took the electoral votes from six deep southern states, ranging in a line from Arkansas to South Carolina, as well as the neighboring northeastern states of Massachusetts and Rhode Island. Even the state of New York, where Smith had been born, lived and served as governor, narrowly went to Hoover. The final electoral college results were astounding, with Hoover securing a whopping 444 votes to Smith's paltry 87. In terms of the popular vote, the disparity continued with Hoover notching 58.3 percent to Al Smith's 40.8 percent.[180]

In Wisconsin, which shared a southeastern border with Hoover's native state of Iowa, the Republican Party's wave had been nearly as profound. Hoover won Wisconsin's thirteen electoral votes by receiving 53.52 percent of the state's popular vote to Smith's 44.28 percent.[181] Republicans in the state also won key races for governor and U.S. Senate. Careful examination of the presidential election numbers, however, reveal that Smith had over performed his national numbers in the state, due to the excitement Wisconsin Catholics had for Smith's candidacy. In fact, in cities like Chippewa Falls, where the Catholic population was on par with Protestants, Smith received the most votes. But according to a front-page article in the *Chippewa Herald*, while Smith had indeed carried the city population by a margin of sixty-seven votes, he had been trounced in the rural areas of Chippewa County. In fact, it was the Protestant-dominated townships, including Hallie, Anson, Tilden, Lafayette and Wheaton, that netted Hoover a nearly one-thousand-vote lead over Smith.[182]

President-elect Hoover, who had run a relatively risk-free campaign, mostly associated himself with the economic successes of the Republican presidents directly preceding him. Born the son of a blacksmith in a small cottage in West Branch, Iowa, Hoover was often seen as a self-made man by rural voters. After becoming a wealthy mining engineer, Hoover was internationally famous for helping to feed the starving people of German-occupied Belgium during World War I. This led to Hoover being appointed head of the U.S. Food Administration, where he was lauded for his efforts in stabilizing farm markets and pricing. He finally served as secretary of commerce under Presidential Warren G. Harding.[183]

To rural farmers in Chippewa County, a vote for Hoover would have seemed natural. However, Hoover's ties to the big-business wing of the national Republican Party likely would have given them at least momentary pause. In "progressive Wisconsin," where a growing strain of Republican candidates railed against predatory corporate behavior, proposals for government action to reign in corporations were popular and frequently successful. On the same night as Hoover's big win, in fact, Wisconsin's progressive Republican senator Robert LaFollette Jr. was reelected by an even wider margin. Regardless of his own personal and political opposition to the Klan, like his father, Robert "Fighting Bob" Lafollete Sr., "Young Bob" still beat his opponent in every county in Wisconsin.[184]

Despite the massive electoral gap between the county's rural and urban voters in the 1928 presidential election, it is difficult to prove that the presence of Klan no. 14 was one of the deciding factors in the outcome. What is clear is that Smith's defeat was exactly what the Grey Eagles and the WKKK had predicted would happen if they successfully mobilized their members by disseminating information that they believed to be true regarding immigrants, alcohol and Catholicism. Both the KKK and the WKKK helped defeat a man who symbolized much of what they feared and hated.

Ironically, the minutes of the November 7 meeting make no overt acknowledgement of Smith or the election. Attending as guests from the

WKKK's Eau Claire Klavern, Excellent Commander Stevens and two unnamed Klanswomen invited the Grey Eagles to attend a future "Hoover Super," which would be held at the Knights of Pythias Hall at 411½ South Barstow Street in downtown Eau Claire. Whether any of the Grey Eagles would attend the dinner event, aptly named to celebrate the election of Hoover, is not known.

Interestingly, much of the substance of the meeting reflected the monetary and maintenance obligations of co-owning and operating the yet-to-be-completed Lake Hallie Klan Hall. After the women added some much-needed revenue from a recent box social, which raised the total balance of their treasury to $69.28 ($991.00 by 2018 standards), the Grey Eagles authorized two major building improvements. The first was the purchase of new lighting for the hall and the second was the application of tar on the Klavern's roof. By 2018 standards, this $501.00 investment in the Klan's tabernacle is major and was possibly made at a time when the women were feeling extremely confident in the future of Klan no. 14.

In many ways, the election of Hoover had reinvigorated the membership. At least in the short run, the attendance was up, and the tabernacle was being improved. On the surface, the future looked promising.

The meeting notes are as follows:

- *Kitchen Committee—Earl, Fisher, Darbe*
- *Sunshine Committee—Hansen*
- *Social Committee—Clara Lange and Bollom*
- *Bills—Flowers—$1.50; Bulletins—$1.35*
- *Discussion on lights and tar for roof. Motion by Borgman, seconded by Bollom…apply $25.00 on lights and $10.00 on tar*
- *Mrs. Stevens, Excellent Commander of Eau Claire, and two others…visiting us tonight, Stevens announced Hoover Supper at Knights of Pythias Hall*
- *50¢…to Hempelman for Sunshine*
- *Discussions…purchase of "Torch"* [WKKK magazine]…
- *Members Present—11*
- *Tess Trainer—Excellent Commander*
- *Mae Connell—Kligrapp (Pro Tem)*[185]

KLONKLAVE NO. 32

November 21, 1928, Wednesday, 9:00 p.m.

The November 21 Klonklave ended up being the last officially opened meeting of 1928, as not enough women showed up at either of the scheduled meetings in December. On this particular evening, the minutes reveal an official acknowledgement of the recent election, as well as how the Grey Eagles responded to a trio of local deaths or tragedies. What isn't specifically mentioned, but what represents an important phase in the meeting history of Klan no. 14, is that this evening was the first of many consecutive Klonklaves to be held in the family home of Klanswoman Nettie Bollom. From November 1928 through April 1929, the two-story Bollom home, located at 122 West Birch Street near downtown Chippewa Falls, would serve as the women's temporary Klavern until the Lake Hallie Klan Hall was finished.

Shortly after officially opening the night's proceedings, the women in attendance decided to reveal the new location of their Klavern meetings to Klanswoman Mary Hempelman. For the entire year of 1928, Mary hadn't attended any of the scheduled meetings or paid her quarterly dues. Despite her delinquency, which was likely rooted in the unfortunate circumstances surrounding the failing health of her mother, the women sent flowers to Mary upon hearing the news of her mother's death. With more than eight months to come to terms with the loss of her mother, and likely energized by the perception of success enjoyed by the WKKK over the recent election results, it appeared that Mary was ready to rejoin her sisters in Klavern.

The return of a once-dues-paying member was certainly welcome news to the treasurer of Klan no. 14, Klabee Olga Smock, as well as Excellent Commander Tess Trainer. Although each member paid the WKKK \$1.50 in quarterly dues, the net quarterly profit that was kept within the local Klavern was \$0.80 per Grey Eagle. The remaining \$0.70 went to the national (\$0.45) and state (\$0.25) levels of the WKKK organization in the form of a Klecktoken, or tax. By 2018 standards, a dues-paying Mary Hempelman would contribute a local Klavern profit of \$11.40 each quarter, or \$45.60 annually.

In addition to the financial resources that were to be gained by the return of Klanswoman Hempelman, the women of Klan no. 14 reported that they had earned \$18.20 from a recent basket social (\$260.00 by 2018 standards). In what was likely seen as a potentially more lucrative opportunity for

Home of Ormal and Nettie Bollom at 112 West Birch Street in Chippewa Falls. *Photo by author.*

growth, the minutes report that the recently organized Women's Club of Lake Hallie, which had several Grey Eagles its membership, including Klanswomen Emma Nihart and Eva Earl, had paid $1.20 for use of the Lake Hallie Klan Hall ($17.20 by 2018 standards). If this could be replicated with other organizations and Protestant church groups, the Grey Eagles could generate a continuous revenue stream that didn't have to come from their own pocketbooks. In a last piece of reassuring financial news, Klanswoman Clark reported a total kitchen profit of $138.29 ($1,980.00 by 2018 standards), which likely included the money raised from food sales at the various socials and "lunches" that were prepared, served and purchased by the members on meeting nights. Financially speaking, 1928 was ending on a very encouraging trend line.

Unfortunately, a trio of deaths left the Grey Eagles reaching out to comfort people connected to the organization. The first unexpected death was the passing of a sixty-five-year-old Chippewa Falls resident named Ada Gillette. Referred to as "Diane's Aunt Ada" in the meeting minutes, Ada Gillette had taught public school at Chestnut Grade School in Chippewa Falls for more than thirty-four years.[186] Although Gillette was not a known member of WKKK, the Grey Eagles' support for public schools made the acknowledgement of her death a priority. Gillette's funeral, which took place in the parlor of her home, located on West Hill at 262 Coleman Street, received a floral arrangement with a card expressing the condolences of Klan no. 14.[187] None of the members were the Diane who was referenced in the minutes.

A second nonmember who received a funerary arrangement from the Grey Eagles was Chippewa Falls resident Bena Lynn. In a horrific accident that covered the front page of the newspaper, thirteen-year-old Lorston Lynn was killed as a result of an automobile hit and run. While helping push a broken-down Studebaker up the Main Street hill in front of Holy Ghost Church on the southside of the river, the teenager was fatally struck by an unknown driver speeding up the hill. As the boy lay dying in the street, the driver sped off and was never heard from again. The women sent a funerary arrangement to the Lynn family, who held the funeral at their home at 631 Wilson Street.[188] While the Sunshine Fund had historically been used to express get-well or condolence messages to people associated with the Grey Eagles, no evidence has surfaced that connects either Ada Gillette or Lorston's mom, Bena Lynn, to Klan no. 14. It's conceivable that the members were simply trying to be good citizens as they reacted to deaths in their community.

The final tragedy that commanded a response from the women was the death of Klanswoman Adella Ellsworth's seventy-one-year-old father."[189] The Ellsworth family also received a floral arrangement expressing the Klan's condolences. In response to the outpouring of support by the community, all three families published thank-you notes in the *Chippewa Herald*.

Before this meeting came to an end, two form letters were read congratulating the women for protecting the presidency from a devout Catholic who was pro-immigrant and favored the legalization of alcohol. The first was composed by Imperial Commander Robbie Gill-Comer and the other was crafted by Imperial Representative Mary J. Bishop.

Even though Klan no. 14 did not meet during December, several Grey Eagles remained socially active throughout the rest of 1928. Meeting in the Odd Fellows Hall in downtown Chippewa Falls, at 9 West Spring Street, the Women's Relief Corps met to elect its officers for the upcoming year. On December 10, the WRC appointed the following Klanswomen officers: Myra Ayers (president), Henrietta Tracy (treasurer) and Tess Trainer (chaplain). In addition, Adella Ellsworth, Henrietta Tracy and Tess Trainer were selected as local delegates to the WRC's state convention. Whether the other members of the WRC were aware of these women's Klan memberships cannot be definitively proven.

The meeting notes are as follows:

- *...let Hempelman know where we now meet...*
- *$1.20 from the Women's Club of Hallie for use of the Klavern, Basket Social—making $19.40. Flowers for Diane's Aunt Ada—$1.50—and Bulletins—$1.35, there is $13.93 in the bank...$38.80 to be banked, $25.00 turned over for lights, $10.00 for roofing, and $7.00 for taxes...total expenses of $42.00*
- *...$1.50 flowers for Bena Lynn's little boy, a motion by Smock and seconded by Strong...carried*
- *Greeting from Robbie Gill-Comer for our election victory...also letter from Klanswoman Mary Bishop*
- *Members Present—10*
- *Tess Trainer—Excellent Commander*
- *Myrtle Hansen—Kligrapp (Pro Tem)*[190]

3

1929

Klonklave No. 33

January 2, 1929, Wednesday, 9:00 p.m.

For the Grey Eagles, 1929 was off to a promising start—they would soon be governed by a new Protestant president. Their first meeting of the year was a mixture of both old business and new. Christmas greetings from national Imperial Commander Robbie Gill-Comer and Wisconsin Realm Commander Edith M. Hunt were read.

The women also decided to purchase a ceremonial torch that consisted of a decorative black wooden shaft donned with a metal reservoir that was used to hold heating oil. A lit torch was an accessory that was used during many of Klavern's rituals and ceremonies, as outlined with the WKKK's Kloran handbook.[191] At a cost of $3.00 ($42.90 by 2018 standards), the torch was the last item that the Grey Eagles needed to complete the Klavern's regalia.

Arguably, the most consequential topic of the evening was the resignation of the Klavern's Kligrapp, Bernice Lekvin. Though she had not been present at any meetings in the fall, Bernice's signature was found prominently on the "Kligrapp's Monthly Reports" through the month of September, and sporadically on others through December. This one-page form was used by the secretary to document the names of the women who had paid their dues, as well as how much Klecktoken the WKKK national headquarters could expect to receive.[192]

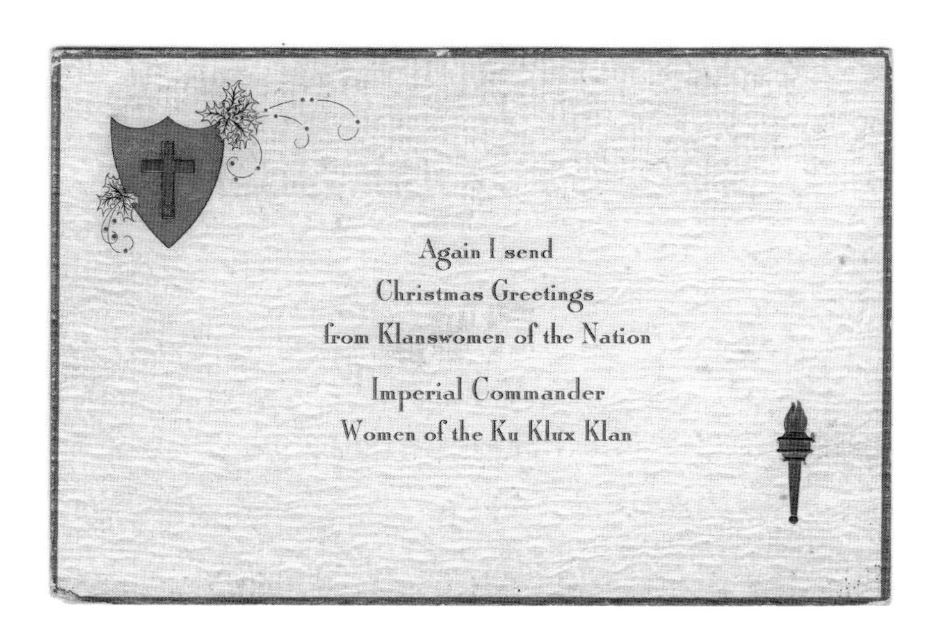

Above: Christmas card from Imperial Commander Robbie Gill-Comer, circa 1929, *Author's collection.*

Right: Shown in her 1923 college graduation photo, Bernice Lekvin was one of the youngest members of the Grey Eagles. *Private collection.*

Mary Bernice Ayers was born on March 26, 1904, in Adams County, Wisconsin, to Harvey and Myra Ayers. The family moved to Chippewa Falls when she was ten, and she married the love of her life, Kahny Lekvin, on September 24, 1927. According to data provided by the United States census, the newlywed couple owned a house on the city's East Hill at 208 Church Street, which was ironically in the shadow of the city's Notre Dame Catholic Church and parsonage.[193] While Kahny worked for the Soo Line Railroad as a yard clerk, Bernice earned an education degree from the Eau Claire Normal School and worked as a public school teacher for some time.

At the age of twenty-four, Bernice was the second-youngest dues-paying member and was well below the 43.5 average age of the group's membership. What she did have in common with the other women was an insatiable appetite for community involvement. Throughout her life, Bernice was active in the Methodist Church, including internal groups, such as the Ladies Aid, Methodist Circle, Church Women United and the Women's Society of Christian Service. She also served alongside several of her Klan sisters in the area's Women's Relief Corps.

Despite her ongoing financial commitment to the Grey Eagles, the birth of her son Owen on September 17, 1928, made Bernice shy away from much of the work and responsibilities associated with the secretary's position.[194] Klan no. 14 chose Adella Ellsworth to take over the role. The rest of the meeting saw the women invest in a set of fifty dinner platters for the nearly completed Lake Hallie Klan Tabernacle and schedule their next box social fundraiser at the home of Nettie Bollom.

The meeting notes are as follows:

- *Christmas Greetings...National/State Offices...*
- *Torch...each Klan supposed to purchase one, motion by Borgman, seconded by Tracy that we buy...carried*
- *Kligrapp Lekvin sent in resignation...Adella Ellsworth appointed...*
- *New business...take money from treasury to buy platters...motion by Kopischkie, seconded by Bollom...buy fifty platters at $0.05 each, carried*
- *Box Social...home of Bollom on Wednesday night...*
- *Members Present*—[Not given]
- *Tess Trainer—Excellent Commander*
- *Adella Ellsworth—Kligrapp*[195]

Klonklave No. 34

January 16, 1929, Wednesday, 9:15 p.m.

In this installment of the minutes, several of the members of Klan no. 14 were reported to be sick. With the harshness of winter in full swing, the average temperature on this day was a bone-chilling 5.5 degrees Fahrenheit.[196] Notes of sunshine, or get-well-soon cards, were mailed to each sick woman. Adella Ellsworth likely viewed her new role as secretary as a way to take her mind off her father's passing.

For the next fundraiser, the women chose a Hard Times Party theme. Popular between the Panic of 1893 and the stock market crash in October 1929, Hard Times Parties became evidence of an emerging and growing "middle class with time and money to spare." Instead of having the women attend the social wearing their finest clothing of "silks and satins," the women were expected to dress down for the occasion in their "dresses made of cheap cotton." The idea was to come as you were and donate the money you saved on clothes to charity.[197] Excellent Commander Tess Trainer, who lived on far eastern side of Catholic Hill in Chippewa Falls, volunteered to host the event.

The meeting notes are as follows:

- *...letters read from National Office...new password given...*
- *...illness reported...sunshine sent: Hempelman, Dittmar, Connell, Darbe*
- *..."Hard Times Party" Friday February 1st at the home of Trainer, carried*
- *Members Present—7*
- *Tess Trainer—Excellent Commander*
- *Adella Ellsworth—Kligrapp*[198]

Klonklave No. 35

January 30, 1929, Wednesday, 9:00 p.m.

Aside from their ongoing preparations for the upcoming Hard Times Party fundraiser, the January 30 meeting saw the Grey Eagles correcting procedural mistakes made while replacing their secretary. When the women of Klan no.

14 accepted Bernice Lekvin's resignation, they did not follow the procedures of replacement as outlined within the Constitution and Laws of the Women of the Ku Klux Klan. Instead of appointing a replacement, which is what Excellent Commander Tess Trainer had done with Adella Ellsworth, the constitution required a three-step process: form a nominating committee, entertain nomination requests by paper ballot and, finally, conclude with a vote by the members in attendance.[199] Trainer, who was normally reliable with the group's adherence to official protocol, promptly corrected the mistake after the Wisconsin Realm Office pointed out the error.

After the group appropriately elected Adella Ellsworth as its secretary, the women decided to purchase blankets for a family facing financial hardship. In Wisconsin, where the low temperatures in January average 16 degrees Fahrenheit,[200] bedding would go a long way.

The meeting notes are as follows:

- *State Office informed...election of Kligrapp not in accord with Constitution...decided to reelect*
- *Report...poor family needing bedding...decided to buy blankets. Motion by Bollom, seconded by Tracy. Tracy and Card...to buy blankets*
- *Members Present—8*
- *Tess Trainer—Excellent Commander*
- *Adella Ellsworth—Kligrapp*[201]

Klonklave No. 36

February 13, 1929, Wednesday, 8:30 p.m.

On the morning of the February 13, the *Chippewa Herald* reported on the unexpected death of a well-known man named Frank B. Chase. Lauded as a "Pioneer Chippewa Falls Resident," who arrived in 1862, seventy-three-year-old Chase had unexpectedly died as the result of a stroke. Although he had worked as Eagle Point Township's assessor, the vast majority of residents knew him as the superintendent of the apple, honey and flower exhibits at the annual Northern Wisconsin State Fair in Chippewa Falls.[202] Out of a desire to show courtesy and respect, although it's likely that the Methodist Church–going Chase was active in the men's Klan, the Grey Eagles took a side collection to pay for a funerary floral arrangement. As the newspaper noted the day after his funeral, "The many banks of floral tributes at the bier were tributes of high esteem in which the pioneer was held."[203]

The women went on to decide that only those who attended the biweekly meetings would receive copies of the Klavern's bulletins. This was a double-edged sword for the Grey Eagles. On one hand, they would save money with the reduction in mailings. On the other hand, the group ran the risk of disconnecting from its more casual members.

The meeting notes are as follows:

- *Communications read...*
- *...flowers for Mr. Chase...*
- *Hansen...motion that members must be present...to get bulletins...carried*
- *Members Present—8*
- *Tess Trainer—Excellent Commander*
- *Adella Ellsworth—Kligrapp*[204]

Klonklave No. 37

March 27, 1929, Wednesday, 8:30 p.m.

The winter of 1929 had been especially harsh. On March 11, the *Chippewa Herald* reported "Fear February Death Rate May Exceed that of January," as the Register of Deeds reported that "influenza and pneumonia [had] swept through the county" and had been credited with the spike in the county's death rate. Sixty-eight deaths were recorded in January, while the unfinished tally for February already listed sixty-two deceased. In the first two months, Chippewa County was averaging more than two deaths per day.[205] The foreboding conditions kept the Grey Eagles from meeting at the start of the month.

In response to the winter's effects, the Grey Eagles felt compelled to assist another family in need by purchasing a set of blankets. The family of Lorenzo and Amelia Butterfield, who lived at 728 West Elm Street in Chippewa Falls, was upended by recent events. Forty-six-year-old Lorenzo, who worked as a farm laborer, had been sick for more than a year. As the family struggled to make ends meet, Lorenzo died on March 11. His forty-three-year-old widow, Amelia, was left to raise and provide for their seven surviving children, ranging in age from two to fourteen.[206] At this meeting, Mary Card was reimbursed for the money she had spent to purchase the bedding for the Butterfields.

The Grey Eagles were in the midst of their most consequential political and cultural fight since the presidential election of 1928. Since the passage of Prohibition in 1920, the ban on the "manufacture, sale, or transportation of intoxicating liquors" had proven difficult to enforce.[207] In 1921, as a way for the state to validate the national ban and assist with its enforcement, Wisconsin enacted its own Severson Prohibition Act. The state law reaffirmed the ban of alcohol in Wisconsin's borders by requiring state police, county sheriffs and local police officers to enforce the ban on alcohol. Unfortunately, the state law proved difficult to enforce as well.

According to Wisconsin's Prohibition commissioner Ronald Dixon, several counties had not been consistent in their enforcement of the Severson Act. While he praised Eau Claire County for "judiciously" carrying out the law, the commissioner refused to say the same about neighboring Chippewa County. Dixon was adamant that an increase in state aid to the counties would improve the ban's success. Whether it was a rural county sheriff's deputy or an urban city's police department, all corners of the state needed more money to increase manpower. Dixon, who painted a bleak assessment of the status of the Severson Act, was adamant that the ban's future could and should be saved.[208]

While the KKK and the WKKK had won their national cultural and political war against Catholicism and Al Smith, their continued attempts to keep Wisconsin alcohol-free was arduous. Too many rural and urban citizens felt immune from the punishment associated with the prohibitions against alcohol. In an attempt to gauge public opinion on the illegality of alcohol, the Wisconsin state legislature scheduled two referendum questions for April 2, 1929:

> *1. Shall...Severson Act... be repealed?*
> *2. Shall...Severson Act...be amended so the state shall not arrest or fine anyone for the manufacture, sale or possession of beer...not more than 2.75% alcohol by weight?*[209]

For many of the Grey Eagles who were also active in the Woman's Christian Temperance Union (WCTU), including Tess Trainer, Lillie Clem, Belle Nelson and Nettie Bollom, the referendum was a call to arms. From the Klan's perspective, a yes vote meant that Wisconsin would

Both the WCTU and WKKK fought to prevent states from undermining the national prohibition of intoxicating liquors, circa 1920. *Author's collection.*

purposely defy the Eighteenth Amendment, which would open the state to fraud, corruption and near limitless acts of illegal behavior. A member of the Eau Claire City Council warned, "This is not a wet or dry issue at all. The real issue is one of upholding law and the Constitution of the United States."

Those in favor of repealing Prohibition also viewed the vote in larger social terms. Milwaukee Socialist state senator Thomas Duncan argued that if the referendum was defeated, the "state will be delivered over, bodily, to the Ku Klux Klan and the Anti-Saloon League, to do as they will with it."[210] In less than one week, members of the Grey Eagles and all of the eligible men and women of Wisconsin, would set the state on one of two drastically divergent courses.[211]

The meeting notes are as follows:

- *Communications read...*
- *Kitchen Committee...Borgman, Dittmar, Card*
- *Motion...Butterfield blankets. $2.34, carried*
- *Severson Law...how to vote April 2nd*
- *Members Present—10*
- *Tess Trainer—Excellent Commander*
- *Mary Clark—Kligrapp (Pro Tem)*[212]

Klonklave No. 38

April 24, 1929, Wednesday, 8:45 p.m.

It had been nearly a month since the Grey Eagles had their last meeting and exactly twenty-two days since the April 2 election. Considering the results from the statewide referendum on repealing the Severson Act, it's plausible to assume that disappointment and disillusionment may have played a role in the women not getting together. The *Eau Claire Leader* reported, "State Votes Wet by Huge Majority—Repeal of Dry Law Favored by 125,000 Margin."[213]

The electorate's response to the first question on whether Wisconsin should repeal the state's Severson Act was a resounding yes, with 64 percent of statewide residents voting to repeal the state's ban on alcohol. On the second question of allowing beer with 2.75 percent alcohol without penalty, statewide voters chose yes by a similar margin. In response, the Wisconsin state legislature voted to repeal the state's ban on alcohol, which left Prohibition enforcement almost exclusively to federal authorities. As a result, the number of Wisconsinites who manufactured, sold, possessed and consumed alcoholic beverages exploded.[214]

Despite the results of the election, Klan no. 14 soldiered on with club business. First, the women decided to buy back the robe of Emma Klages. She had decided to leave the organization for unspecified reasons and hadn't paid her dues since September 1928.

Born in 1884 in Wisconsin, Emma Klemke was the daughter of two German immigrants. After marrying Gustave Klages, the couple raised their two children in a rented house at 315 East Columbia Street, on the East Hill in the city of Chippewa Falls. Gustave was a carpenter in the local mill, while Emma worked as a waitress in a downtown café.[215] In addition to her membership in the Chippewa Falls WKKK, Emma was a frequent participant in the Ladies Aid club of her Lutheran church. While one can only speculate why Emma chose to leave the Grey Eagles, newspaper accounts hint that her expanded duties as an officer within the Woman's Relief Corps likely played a role.[216]

One of the final lines in the minutes seems to gloss over a historic moment for the women's Klavern by nonchalantly stating, "No meeting. Moved to Hallie." The women had decided that May 10 would be set aside for moving all of the order's belongings to the new tabernacle building in the nearby Township of Lake Hallie. Since the previous November, all of Klan no. 14's meetings had been hosted at the family home of Klanswoman Nettie Bollom at 122 West Birch Street, which was located near downtown Chippewa Falls. With the move to the new Lake Hallie Klan Tabernacle, the women would now be meeting in a more rural and secluded setting.

The meeting notes are as follows:

- *...pay Mrs. Klages $2.00 for robe*
- *No meeting, moved to Hallie*
- *Members Present—8*
- *Tess Trainer—Excellent Commander*
- *Mary Clark—Kligrapp (Pro Tem)*[217]

Klonklave No. 39

May 24, 1929, Wednesday, 8:45 p.m.

After more than a year and half of planning and fundraising, the men and women of the Chippewa Falls Klans finally had their own stand-alone meeting place. This installment of the minutes reveals that the May 24 Klonklave was the first regular meeting held at the new Lake Hallie Klan Tabernacle. Located roughly five miles southwest from the original meeting place in downtown Chippewa Falls, the new tabernacle was situated midway between the cities of Chippewa Falls and Eau Claire.

In selecting a suitable property for the new Klavern, the Wisconsin Realm Office offered several considerations. The building should be "well-lighted, well-ventilated" and large enough to seat about "one-half" of a Klan's membership. The property should "not be too public," nor should it contain any "Klan name, sign or other emblem," as "its identity should be kept secret as far as possible." Most importantly, the Klans were instructed "not to own their own Klavern" buildings, as it "doesn't pay" from a financial investment standpoint. All chartered Klan organizations were encouraged to rent a building from a trusted property owner whose location was fully insured.[218]

Situated near the perimeter of an eighty-acre parcel of land that was once owned by Lake Hallie farmer and German immigrant Julius Sippel, the Klan's new tabernacle began as a wooden horse stable on the corner of the Sippel's Farm. The modified building was accessed by an unassuming dirt road that ventured two blocks east of the one-lane concrete road, called Joles Road or old U.S. Highway 53. The wooded rural township site offered seclusion and privacy for secret meetings and rituals, while retaining convenient access by automobile. Situated away from the city and the general public, the Klanswomen felt more comfortable wearing their robes.

According to a county deed, the parcel containing the tabernacle was sold for one dollar to Harry and Violet Cale of Lake Hallie on March 1, 1929.[219] Harry opened a mechanic's business called Midway Garage on the western corner of the property, while the Klan building occupied the eastern side, roughly two blocks away. The location of Cale's garage provided a convenient lookout to monitor any suspicious motorists who might venture off the concrete road toward the tabernacle.[220]

While no documentation exists on how and why this particular parcel and structure was chosen as the new tabernacle, at least one of Julius Sippel's children had a direct connection to the hooded order. Emma Nihart, born

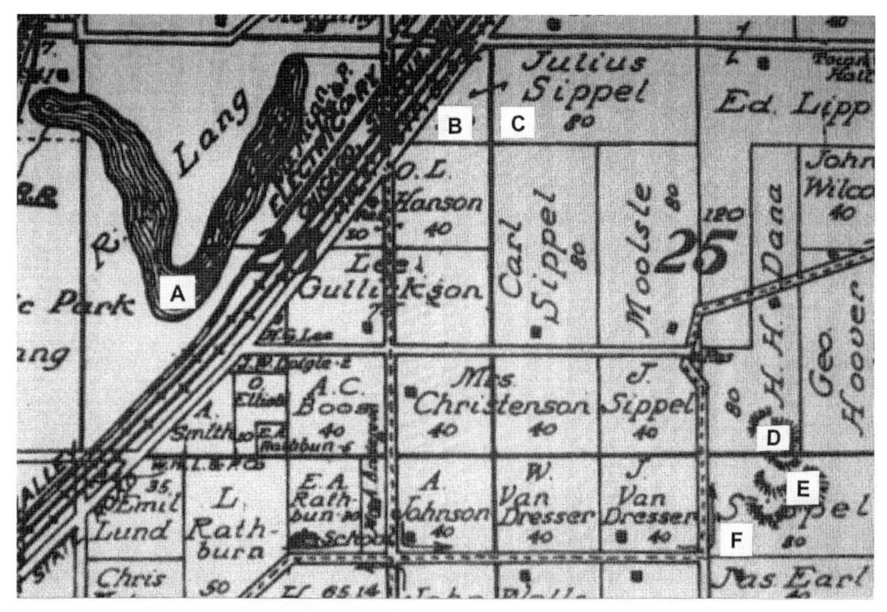

A. Lake Hallie
B. Klan Tabernacle (Holiday Stationstores/Burger King Restaurant)
C. Klan Field #1 (Wal-Mart Supercenter and other retail businesses)
D. Dana's Bluff
E. Round Top - Cross Burning Hill (Municipal Water Tower)
F. Klan Field #2 (Private farm land)

Map of Klan-related locations in the Village of Lake Hallie. *Author's collection.*

Men, women and children from the Eau Claire Klans pose for a photo in Klan Field in Lake Hallie. *Chippewa Valley Museum, 1926.*

to Julius and Lucinda Sippel in 1889, married Jacob Nihart in a Methodist ceremony in 1920.[221] In addition to being a mother of three children and a dues-paying member of Klan no. 14, she was also active in the Hallie Woman's Club,[222] and hosted a handful of the group's meetings in her family's home. When Julius died in August 1927, his land was divided among several surviving children, including Emma.[223]

Though it had taken nearly two years to complete the Lake Hallie Klan Hall, only eight women attended the first regular Klonklave. For those in attendance, there was critical business to complete, as the Grey Eagles were scheduled to host the WKKK's Klonverse, or convention, for Province no. 2. In addition to Tess Trainer, Olga Smock, Mary Clark, Eva Earl and Emma Dittmar were voted to be the group's four delegates, or Kleepers, to represent the Klavern at the convention.

The meeting notes are as follows:

- *First meeting...at Hallie Hall*
- *...nominations for Kleepers:*
  - *1=Smock*
  - *2=Mary Clark*
  - *3=Earl*
  - *4=Dittmar*
- *Members Present—8*
- *Tess Trainer—Excellent Commander*
- *Myrtle Hansen—Kligrapp (Pro Tem)*[224]

KLONKLAVE NO. 40

June 5, 1929, Wednesday, 8:45 p.m.

In the lead-up to the second meeting in the new Lake Hallie Klan Tabernacle, the Grey Eagles received an urgent letter from the WKKK's Imperial Headquarters. Imperial Commander Robbie Gill-Comer was informing all of her Klans that the ultraconservative *Fellowship Forum* newspaper was in dire need of postage stamps to mail literature promoting an upcoming public school bill in Congress. The WKKK, which was still committed to national legislation guaranteeing every child a "complete grammar school education with a well-prepared teacher," was supportive of the passage of the Robsion-Capper Bill. In her letter, Gill-Comer acknowledged that the *Fellowship Forum*'s editing manager, Jams S. Vance, had implored her for the WKKK's assistance. Vance explained that they did not have enough funds to "carry the message to the public" and hoped that each WKKK unit could donate. Though the Grey Eagles had previously given money for the *Forum*'s radio station, the women decided against sending assistance.[225]

In a second letter from the Imperial Commander's office, the date, location and time of the WKKK's national convention was revealed. The letter stated, "During the national Klonvokation, June 28th and 29th, 1929, the Palmer House, Chicago, Illinois, will be headquarters for the WKKK."[226]

While none of the women from the Chippewa Falls unit attended the national convention, several did attend the Wisconsin Realm's Provincial no. 2 gathering that was just two days later. In addition to Trainer and the four delegates elected at the last meeting, Agnes Clark and Emma Nihart were elected as alternate Kleepers for the Friday event. The members also decided which women would hold Klavern offices for the upcoming year. Of particular interest was the nomination of Nettie Bollom as the new Excellent Commander, as Tess Trainer was looking forward to stepping away from the position to work as the secretary.

The meeting notes are as follows:

- *Nominating Committee...*
- *Chairman Agnes Clark, Nihart, Card*
- *Alternate Kleepers:*
    - *1=Agnes Clark*
    - *2=Emma Nihart*
- *Nominating Committee reported...*
    - *Klaliff=Clark*
    - *Klockard=Connell*
    - *Kludd=Clem*
    - *Kligrapp=Trainer*
    - *Klabee=Tracy*
    - *Kladd=Earl*
    - *Klarogo=Darbe*
    - *Klexter=Tracy*
    - *Night Hawk=Card*
    - *Excellent Commander=Nettie Bollom*
- *Members Present—Unknown*
- *Tess Trainer—Excellent Commander*
- *Henrietta Tracy—Kligrapp (Pro Tem)*[227]

KLONKLAVE NO. 41 (SPECIAL KLONVERSE OF PROVINCE NO. 2)

June 7, 1929, Friday, 2:45 p.m.

The special meeting of Province no. 2 of the Wisconsin Realm of the WKKK was the second annual western provincial meeting held at in the Township of Lake Hallie. Just like in 1928, neither local newspaper was made aware of the event. Unlike the last year, however, the women in attendance marveled at the newly completed tabernacle. In addition to the Kleepers who represented Klan no. 14, delegates from Cornell, Menomonie and Eau Claire attended. While the provincial meeting had gained the attendance of a new batch of delegates from Menomonie (Dunn County), there were no Kleepers present from Douglas, Pierce or La Crosse counties. While it's possible that those Klans chose not to send delegates, it is conceivable that lagging membership numbers played a role as well. Even though a respectable twenty-two Klanswomen were in attendance, it was noticeably fewer than the thirty-plus who attended the same event in 1928.

Much of the provincial meeting's agenda revolved around deciding who would attend the State Klorero on behalf of the western district. From the Grey Eagles, Agnes Clark was the number one delegate, while Myrtle Hansen was named alternate. A Mrs. Wilson from Eau Claire received the highest honor of all, as she was chosen to be the Province no. 2 delegate to the WKKK's National Klonvokation in Chicago.

The last order of business was a group brainstorming of strategies to expand fundraisers, increase meeting attendance and retain existing membership. The Kleeper from Krimson Kross Klan in Menomonie suggested that each Klan should adopt its own biweekly "social day," similar to those used by the religious-based Ladies Aid Clubs, and headline a program, sermon or picnic lunch to increase attendance and Klavern profits. Another suggestion called for each Klanswoman to vow to take $0.50 ($7.15 by 2018 standards) and invest in something not involving "moonshine," such as "sewing, baking, or any honest way," and sell their creations to make profit for their Klavern.

On the reoccurring problem of low attendance, which directly led to inconsistency in membership dues collections, the women decided that they should consider aligning meeting nights with the men and have each woman retake the Klan oath of allegiance. Although they had a discussion about the feasibility of lowering the cost of the quarterly dues "if possible,"

Klan gathering in Lake Hallie, circa 1929. *Author's collection.*

Klan crosses in Lake Hallie, circa 1929. *Author's collection.*

Grey Eagles near Chippewa Falls, circa 1929. *Author's collection.*

nearly all of the women discussed the need for getting more money into their Klavern's treasuries, not less. In the end, the women adjourned with an upbeat attitude despite their financial and membership issues. The mantra moving forward was "forget how to say I can't do something or I can't do that."

The meeting notes are as follows:

- *Province No. 2 meeting...Lake Hallie Klavern...*
- *Meeting called to order...Great Klaliff...singing of "America." Prayer by Chippewa Kludd*
- *Motion by Blanchard (Menomonie), seconded by Livermore (Cornell)...send greetings to Realm Representative Bishop, carried*
- *Nominations for Kleepers and alternates...Klorero at Menomonie, June 14th...*

1=Agnes Clark; Alternate=Myrtle Hansen
2=Jacobs; Alternate=Blanchard
3=Wilson; Alternate=Winters
4=Livermore. Alternate=Livermore given privilege to send substitute...
5=Winters; Alternate=Peterson

- *Nominations for National Delegate*
  - *Delegate: Wilson (Eau Claire, WI), elected*
  - *Alternate: Winters, elected*
- *Since Kluxers are unable to hold sales on most anything.. vowed to take 50¢ and invest it in some way...baking, sewing, or any honest way (unlike moonshine, etc)*
- *...Menomonie said they have a "Social Day" every other Sunday. Picnic dinners, program or sermon...like (Ladies) Aid...*
- *...retake the oath, meet when men meet, lower dues if possible, and each one forget how to say 'I can't do that or I don't know how'*
- *...closed at 4:40 PM with prayer...*
- *Members Present—22*
- *Tess Trainer—Excellent Commander*
- *Unknown—Kligrapp*[228]

KLONKLAVE NO. 42

June 19, 1929, Wednesday, 9:00 p.m.

Five days earlier, on Flag Day, the WKKK's Wisconsin Realm hosted its annual State Klorero in nearby Menomonie. The Krimson Kross Klan no. 32, which had opened its own Klavern less than one year prior, was anxious to play host to Klanswomen from all over the state. Agnes Clark attended as an elected delegate, representing her fellow Grey Eagles. Unfortunately, no evidence has surfaced regarding the happenings of the event.

Since none of the Grey Eagles were planning to attend the event in Chicago, they would have to wait for the delegate from Eau Claire, Mrs. Wilson, to make a full report upon her return.

Before the June 19 meeting came to a close, one notable decision was reached. A motion was made by Myrtle Hansen to postpone the election of the remaining officers until the next meeting, including the vital position of Excellent Commander. Ironically, the member who seconded the motion was Nettie Bollom, who everyone expected would be Tess Trainer's replacement. It's possible that Nettie was having second thoughts about taking on all of the responsibilities associated with the position of Excellent Commander.

The meeting notes are as follows:

- *Motion by Hansen, seconded by Bollom, postpone election of other officers...carried*
- *Members Present—8*
- *Tess Trainer—Excellent Commander*
- *Myrtle Hansen—Kligrapp (Pro Tem)*[229]

KLONKLAVE NO. 43

July 24, 1929, Wednesday, 9:20 p.m.

For reasons not shared within the minutes, the Klonklave scheduled for July 10 never materialized. As a result, Klan no. 14 had gone more than a month since its last official gathering. On this evening, after the Excellent Commander arrived late, three important topics were addressed.

On July 10, 1929, the *Chippewa Herald* had reported on the passing of Mrs. Anna O. Rude, who died at her daughter's home at 318 North Grove Street in Chippewa Falls. Anna, a Norwegian-born Lutheran immigrant, came to the United States as little girl in 1871. The *Herald* referred to her as a "fine specimen of the old Northern Wisconsin type of pioneer who sixty years ago enjoyed tallow or kerosene lights and ox-team transportation as exceptional luxuries of the times."[230] Even though Rude herself was not a member of the Grey Eagles, both her daughter, Mary Clark née Rude, and her granddaughter Agnes Butler née Clark were. To pay tribute to the matriarch who helped rear two of the most reliable women in their ranks, flowers were purchased for her funeral.

A second topic was the uncertainty regarding the unfilled Excellent Commander position. Once again, Nettie Bollom shared her apprehensions. Her reluctance to accept the role was likely rooted in natural nervousness. Tess Trainer had set the bar high, and the Grey Eagles had never known a formal leader other than her. By the end of the meeting, Nettie had been voted in as the Klavern's new Excellent Commander.

Finally, the women of Klan no. 14 had received a letter regarding an upcoming visit from the national WKKK's Imperial Klaliff, or vice-president, Anna E. Wilson.[231]

With the possibility that the national vice president might be hosted at the Lake Hallie Klan Tabernacle, Trainer proposed that they schedule a Klonklave for July 31 and then reschedule their future biweekly meetings accordingly.

The meeting notes are as follows:

- *Motion by Hansen, seconded by Borgman,...A. Rude flowers be paid, carried*
- *Motion by Hansen, seconded by Earl, Nettie Bollom accept Excellent Commander, unanimous.*
- *Members Present—13*
- *Tess Trainer—Excellent Commander*
- *Agnes Clark—Kligrapp (Pro Tem)*[232]

Klonklave No. 44

July 31, 1929, Wednesday, 9:00 p.m.

The July 31 Klonklave was attended by eleven members. Though the women hoped to host the national Imperial Klaliff, there is no mention of any visitor or special guest attending the evening's events. Instead, the women carried out the rituals of the annual installation ceremony and officially swore in the newly elected officers for the upcoming year.

Out of all of the positions that needed to be filled, none was more important and vital to the success of the Klavern than the position of leader. According to the minutes, Excellent Commander Nettie Bollom eagerly began her term by scheduling a play and a meatball dinner to continue to raise money. Unfortunately, the women did not leave any information about which play they chose to perform.

The minutes include another veiled reference to the Grey Eagles' growing financial concerns. After Mary Clark thanked the women for sending flowers to her mother's funeral, it was decided that future tributes would consist of "only cards at the time of death to paid-up members." Although the change in the Klavern's sympathy policy would likely end up saving the group money in the short run, it ran the risk of offending sisters during times of need.

The meeting notes are as follows:

- *Mary Clark installing officer...Borgman as Marshall...installed: Connell, A. Clark, Bollom, Darbe, Smock, M. Clark, Borgman, Hansen*
- *Five books sent for the play...prices for the play 35¢ and 15¢. Bollom Chairman of Play Committee*
- *M. Clark thanked the order for flowers...motion by Borgman, seconded by Bollom, to only send cards at the time of death to paid-up members*
- *Meatball supper discussed...*
- *Members Present—11*
- *Tess Trainer—Excellent Commander*
- *Myrtle Hansen—Kligrapp (Pro Tem)*[233]

Klonklave No. 45

August 14, 1929, Wednesday, 8:45 p.m.

In the first Klonklave that Nettie Bollom presided over as Excellent Commander, just six Grey Eagles witnessed the transition. Even the reliable Tess Trainer was not in attendance. The newly elected forty-four-year-old leader would have a less than stellar reign. Not once in any of the eight Klonklaves that she presided over did attendance reach double digits. Nonetheless, Nettie was well known and experienced in the Klavern's routines, as she had served as the Klavern's Kludd, or chaplain, since the group's inception. Nettie could recite the Klavern's prayer from memory and had likely memorized many of Tess's ritual lines from her frequent presence at the meetings. Like Tess, Nettie was a woman of social activism who divided her time into many different causes and organizations within the Chippewa Falls community.

Born on October 21, 1885, Nettie M. Larson was the daughter of two Scandinavian immigrants. Her father, Andrew Larson, was from Denmark, while her mother, Helen Westly, had arrived from Norway.[234] Nettie was born and raised on a farm near Osseo, Wisconsin, located some thirty-one miles south of the Lake Hallie Klan Tabernacle. On November 19, 1907, shortly after she turned thirty-two years old, Nettie Larson married the love of her life, Ormal Bollom, in a church in Osseo.[235]

Ormal and Nettie moved to Chippewa Falls and opened Bollom Jewelers at 7 West Central Street.[236] Often advertising high-end products such as Elgin and Speidel watches and accessories, Ormal and Nettie operated the jewelry store for more than thirty-four years. By the time Nettie was elevated to Excellent Commander, she had given birth to five children and was stepmother to one daughter from Ormal's first marriage.

In addition to her Klan activities, Nettie was a high-ranking member of the Chippewa Falls chapter of the Royal Neighbors of America. She served as the group's oracle, or president, at the same time as she was Excellent Commander. In addition to fighting for women's suffrage, the Royal Neighbors sought economic security for women in the form of life insurance. At a time that predated social welfare programs like Social Security, social clubs like the Royal Neighbors became major venues for women like Nettie to access affordable life insurance. Without these types of offerings, the death of a husband could lead a widow into a life of hardship or complete destitution. Nettie wasn't alone in her involvement in the Royal Neighbors, as Klanswomen Lillie Clem, Mary Card and Grace and Henrietta Tracy joined her in this social fraternity.

In addition to her connections with the Royal Neighbors, Nettie's objections to alcohol brought her to serve in the Woman's Christian Temperance Union. Along with Tess Trainer, Lillie Clem, Belle Nelson and several other Grey Eagles, dual membership in the WKKK and the WCTU allowed these women to fight alcohol on two fronts. While it's not known if Nettie had been a ranking officer in the WCTU, her devout Protestant faith, personal confidence and refined public speaking prowess made her the ideal successor to Tess Trainer as Excellent Commander.[237]

The meeting notes are as follows:

- *Communications read...*
- *...play discussed...*
- *Members Present—6*
- *Nettie Bollom—Excellent Commander*
- *Agnes Clark—Kligrapp (Pro Tem)*[238]

KLONKLAVE NO. 46

September 25, 1929, Wednesday, 8:45 p.m.

A month after their last Klonklave, only five women managed to make an appearance at the September 25 meeting. Those who did attend voted to reward Excellent Commander Nettie Bollom for allowing the Grey Eagles to use her family's home as the group's temporary Klavern. For roughly six months, from November to April, Klan no. 14 had been meeting in the parlor of Nettie's home. Recognizing the inconvenience, as well as the graciousness of her generosity, the women decided that the Klavern would pay Nettie's dues for the last quarter of the year.

As the Grey Eagles continued their efforts to sustain the financial obligations associated with the operation of the Lake Hallie Klan Tabernacle, Bollom announced that the practice for the upcoming theatrical play would take place at the Lake Hallie home of Eva Earl.

The meeting notes are as follows:

- *Vote...give Bollom paid up card for the year for rent at home last winter (November 14 to April 24th)*

- *Basket Social...October 4th, if favorable with the men...Bollom and Trainer to make coffee, bread and meat for extra sandwiches, grab basket for children*
- *Play practice at Earl's...Monday night...*
- *Closed at 9:45 PM...rained hard*
- *Members Present—5*
- *Nettie Bollom—Excellent Commander*
- *Tess Trainer—Kligrapp*[239]

Klonklave No. 47

October 23, 1929, Wednesday, 9:00 p.m.

For the third consecutive month, the Grey Eagles only attended one Klonklave. According to the minutes, the women used this meeting to practice "Kloranic work," or rituals and procedures found within the WKKK's Kloran, in preparation for an assemblage on October 28. If this gathering did occur, no written evidence remains of it.

In a motion made by Kligrapp Tess Trainer and seconded by Mae Connell, the women authorized a payment of $35 ($501 by 2018 standards) in rent to the "Badger Club."[240] While it's possible that the Badger Club was simply the name of the men's Chippewa Falls KKK unit, and thus the majority stakeholders of the Lake Hallie Klan Tabernacle, a fragmented letter written by Tess Trainer reveals more:

> *Dear Klanswoman,*
> *Since we are not wanting to see you give up...to so worthy a cause as... our Klan, we are again asking you to become one in our big family circle, and come to a joint meeting on October 28th with that purpose. That shall be your password of admission. We need you and you need us... we stand, need the support of every Protestant in the land. Let's not be caught, "asleep at the..."*[241]

Badger Club likely reflected an organizational merger that took place between the male and female Chippewa Falls Klan units. Such a partnership would have been seen as a prudent mitigation of several challenges, such as slumping meeting attendance, recurring stress with dues collections and stagnant revenue gathered from competing fundraisers.

Unfortunately, neither Trainer nor the meeting minutes divulge any specifics of the "big family circle" they sought to create. If the Badger Club was indeed an effort to join the men and women's units together, it would have violated the rules and regulations of both the national KKK and WKKK organizations. No standalone documents have surfaced to provide any further insight into the club's activities.

Curiously, the members of the Badger Club must have felt secure using the name. On a few occasions, it appeared as an entry under the "Society—Lodges and Clubs" section of the *Chippewa Herald*. One blurb titled "Enjoy Card and Bunco Party" detailed how members of the "Hallie Badger Club" journeyed to the home of Mr. and Mrs. Martin Connell (Klanswoman Mae Connell and her husband). The members had an enjoyable evening "playing bunco and progressive schmier" with a group of "thirty people from Eau Claire, Chippewa Falls, and Eagle Point." The notice added that a Mr. Earl Hempelman (Klanswoman Mary Hempelman's husband) won the men's first place prize, while the women's champion card player was a Mrs. Jasper Tracy (Klanswoman

Christmas card sent by WKKK Imperial Headquarters, circa 1930. *Author's collection.*

Henrietta Tracy). The society piece concluded by listing all of the guests who had won consolation prizes during the Badger Club's get together, including Klanswomen Agnes Clark and Anna Borgman.[242]

A second piece of evidence that the men and women had merged into the Badger Club is an interview that was conducted by the *Eau Claire Leader Telegram* in 1993. An eighty-nine-year-old resident named Lucille Malom recalled how she and her family would attend the Klan events out of "curiosity and for the chicken." Malom added, "Oh, they served good chicken dinners, those Klan people."[243] Several advertisements in the *Chippewa Herald* also showed the Badger Club hosting similar events at the tabernacle.[244]

Though the Grey Eagles would never again host their own independently run fundraiser, they still maintained separate Klavern finances. Any membership dues paid to the national and state WKKK were kept in the local unit's treasury. Any remaining Klavern dues were to be used for ordering bulletins, postage stamps, other Klavern supplies or the sunshine fund for get-well or sympathy cards. Moving forward, all kitchen profits would go directly into the treasury of the newly formed Badger Club.

The meeting notes are as follows:

- *...bill of $2.59 for play books and postage, allowed*
- *Moved by Trainer, seconded by Connell...pay Badger Club $35.00 rent for the Hall, carried*
- *Practice Kloranic work Sunday...*
- *Members Present—7*
- *Nettie Bollom—Excellent Commander*
- *Tess Trainer—Kligrapp*[245]

Klonklave No. 48

November 6, 1929, Wednesday, 8:45 p.m.

As the seven attending Grey Eagles gathered at the Lake Hallie Klan Hall on November 6, a critical piece of official WKKK business awaited them. In a letter, Edith M. Hunt, the Wisconsin Realm Commander and Imperial Representative, announced that she was calling for a second state Klonverse to be held in each WKKK Wisconsin province. The women in Province no. 1 would meet in Janesville on November 6, while those in Province no. 2 would gather in Menomonie on November 15. The lengthy program included:

Afternoon Session:
12:30 PM...registration
1:30 PM...Assembly
Business Session
Election of Great Officers
Open Forum
Supper...(Served by Menomonie Women)

Evening Session:
8:00 PM...prompt
Joint Meeting...Klanswomen/Klansmen
Special Program
Address by Grand Dragon
Address by Imperial Representative
Benediction[246]

Realm Commander Hunt implored that all members in good standing should "make your plans now, come by car, train, or any way to get there." She encouraged each Klan to invite and bring along members who were delinquent in their dues but made it clear that their involvement would be limited to the dinner and the evening propaganda speeches. In a tactful acknowledgement that the Wisconsin Realm of the WKKK was experiencing some internal dissension, Hunt declared, "That problems of all nature will be brought up at this meeting," and "all suggestions are asked for at this time." She went on to remind the women that these special gatherings needed to be funded by the Klans within their respective provinces and established a twenty-five-cent registration fee for each attendee. Those planning to eat the provided supper were asked to bring money for their meal, and all proceeds would benefit the women of Menomonie's Krimson Kross Klan. Hunt ended her letter in all capital letters, exclaiming, "BE SURE AND LET ALL ROADS LEAD TO YOUR PROVINCE MEETING."[247]

Even though Realm Commander Hunt did not disclose the reason for the emergency gathering, front-page newspaper headlines between October 24 and 29 reveal the culprit. The record-setting stock market crash of 1929 had sent national and global economic markets into freefall. With the country and the world on the brink of a lengthy depression, the convention in Menomonie had been called to address the immediate financial ramifications to the Klan and its members. Unfortunately, the full weight of the crash would be felt for nearly a decade. By 1932, the average stock was worth only 20 percent of its original 1929 value, resulting in billions of dollars of lost investment earnings. By 1933, half of banks across the United States would fail, while unemployment skyrocketed to 30 percent of the eligible workforce.[248] The most drastic economic shift in U.S. history was at hand, and both the KKK and WKKK would suffer its wrath.

Locally, the Grey Eagles made a bold move. Klanswoman Tracy made a motion that the "Women of the Ku Klux Klan sell, to the Badger Club, all property and belongings." All seven women in attendance unanimously agreed and sold the group's posessions (including the regalia, piano and dishes) to the recently formed Badger Club for $25 ($286 by 2018 standards). While the women would continue to hold their own meetings as members of Klan no. 14, both the men and women reached the conclusion that they would need to pool their efforts if they intended to keep the Lake Hallie Klan Tabernacle operational. Although the creation of the "big family circle" had been in the works for at least two weeks, the crash solidified the economic necessity of the move.

The meeting notes are as follows:

1. *Correspondence read...*
2. *Bill of 10¢...two Bill of Sale forms...*
3. *Moved by Tracy, seconded by Clark...sell, to the Badger Club, all property and belongings, unanimous...*
4. *Members Present—7*
5. *Nettie Bollom—Excellent Commander*
6. *Tess Trainer—Kligrapp*[249]

Klonklave No. 49

December 4, 1929, Wednesday, Time Unknown

The specially scheduled Province no. 2 Klonverse in Menomonie came and went without any mention in the minutes. The December 4 Klonklave was filled with mundane business, such as dues collections, a kitchen report and a discussion about postage stamps for mailing bulletins. Meanwhile, an article in the *Eau Claire Leader* had falsely speculated that most Klan organizations around the state had ceased operations, as public Klan spectacles had become increasingly rare. In an article title "Fiery Cross Burned by Milwaukee Klan," the Milwaukee police were openly "wondering if Klansmen had become active again" after a cross burning had been reported in front of a soft drink parlor. Like most other Klan units, the men and women of Chippewa Falls were still active. Due to a growing weariness and skepticism toward the media's coverage of the hooded order, more and more Klans faded into the shadows of strategically located Klaverns in rural Wisconsin.[250]

The meeting notes are as follows:

- *Clark, chairman of the kitchen, gave a report…*
- *Motion…lay the bill for stamps until next meeting, carried*
- *Members Present—7*
- *Nettie Bollom— Excellent Commander*
- *Myrtle Hansen— Kligrapp*[251]

4

1930

Klonklave No. 50

January 1, 1930, Wednesday, 8:00 p.m.

With the formation of the Badger Club and the stock market crash figuring prominently in the direction of the Chippewa Falls Women of the Ku Klux Klan, the minutes of 1930 reveal a much-altered organization. The women would only meet seven times as a gender-segregated unit, and they no longer discussed hosting fundraisers or social events for themselves. Aside from a card featuring Christmas and New Year's greetings from Imperial Headquarters, the major points of discussion for this evening's meeting involved the collection of dues from three of the members.

The meeting notes are as follows:

- *New Year's greeting…Robbie Gill Comer*
- *Members Present—7*
- *Nettie Bollom—Excellent Commander*
- *Myrtle Hansen—Kligrapp (Pro Tem)*[252]

No. 76646

VOID AFTER 12/31/1930

TESS Trainer.

TYPE MEMBERS NAME HERE

Tess Trainer

BEARERS OWN SIGNATURE IN INK

14 Chippewa Falls Wis

KLAN NO. CITY REALM

REALM COMMANDER

Excellent Commander Tess Trainer's membership card, circa 1930. *Private collection.*

Klonklave No. 51

February 5, 1930, Wednesday, Time Unknown

During the February 5 meeting, the Grey Eagles officially received one dollar for the bill of sale from the Badger Club. They also proceeded to purchase office supplies for the Klavern, including dues books, stamps and stationery. Though they had merged with the men's unit, which would replace one of the order's monthly meetings, the women appeared committed to maintaining their own independent ladies-only unit. Their future obligations to the national and state WKKK, however, would be tested almost immediately.

The meeting notes are as follows:

- *Received $1...Bill of Sale from Badger Club*
- *Members Present—7*
- *Nettie Bollom—Excellent Commander*
- *Myrtle Hansen—Kligrapp (Pro Tem)*[253]

Klonklave No. 52

June 18, 1930, Wednesday, 8:50 p.m.

With more than three months passing since the Grey Eagles held a ladies-only Klonklave, much had happened within the WKKK's Realm of Wisconsin. On May 3 and 4, the third annual Klonverse of Province no. 2 took place in Ellsworth. Whether any of the women from Klan no. 14 made the seventy-mile trip west is not known. At the provincial assembly, a list of eight resolutions were agreed on and disseminated in a letter to all of the state's Klans:

1. *Resolved…send greeting to Imperial Commander Robbie Gill-Comer…*
2. *Resolved…send greeting to Mary Jane Bishop…*
3. *Resolved…each write to our Senator in care of Fellowship Forum urging passage of Robsion-Capper Bill…*
4. *Resolved…we work for strict enforcement of Volstead Act*
5. *Resolved…we petition our congressman…for restriction of immigration*
6. *Resolved…we do personal work to increase attendance at…meetings*
7. *Resolved…appreciation…work done by Imperial Representative Edith Hunt*
8. *Resolved…thank the ladies of Ellsworth…entertaining the meeting of Province No. 2*[254]

The Ellsworth Resolutions revealed just how adamant the women remained to the creation of a National Department of Public Education in Washington, D.C., and the continuation of the ongoing national ban on alcohol. Just as notable, two of the resolutions reflect the far-reaching influence of the literature and propaganda of the *Fellowship Forum* publication.[255]

Even though Imperial Representative Edith Hunt stated that all units within Province no. 2 were "requested to adopt above resolutions at their next regular Klonklave," the Grey Eagles would not officially approve the Ellsworth Resolutions until September. Unfortunately for Klan no. 14, a more pressing issue surpassed the importance of the resolutions.

Excellent Commander Nettie Bollom, who had yet to complete an entire year as leader of Klan no. 14, officially tendered her resignation. Although the nine women in attendance ultimately accepted Nettie's resignation, they certainly didn't want to. It seemed that no one who continued attending the meetings wanted to fill her shoes.

One of the women present, Klanswoman Emma Dittmar, looked to her close friend Tess Trainer. Although Emma and her husband, Fred, had been reliable, dues-paying members of both Klan organizations for years, Emma likely didn't see herself as the person to assume the leadership position.

Born to German immigrant parents in 1868, Emma Happle married Fred Dittmar in 1910. Unlike many of her fellow Grey Eagles, Emma did not have a long history of participation in other social clubs. In addition to Klan activities, she was deeply committed to her Presbyterian faith.[256]

Emma and Fred did not have children, and they lived at 739 Mansfield Street on the West Hill of Chippewa Falls.[257] The sixty-one-year-old Emma was listed by the 1930 United States Census as a "homemaker," while Fred worked downtown for the locally prominent A.C. Mason Shoe Company. In an ironic twist that was likely not lost on the Dittmars, Albert C. Mason wasn't just one of the most prominent and affluent citizens in Chippewa Falls, but he was also the patriarch of one of the most high-profile Catholic families in western Wisconsin.

As for Emma's motion to nominate Tess for a reprisal role as Excellent Commander, it was decided to wait until the next meeting since Trainer was already sworn in as secretary.

The meeting notes are as follows:

- *Excellent Commander Bollom tendered resignation...reluctantly accepted*
- *Nominations...new Excellent Commander*
- *Hansen nominated Clark. Refused*
- *Trainer nominated Tracy. Refused*
- *Dittmar nominated Trainer, who has one office. Hansen moved that nominations be tabled until July 2nd...carried*
- *Members Present—9*
- *Nettie Bollom—Excellent Commander*
- *Tess Trainer—Kligrapp*[258]

KLONKLAVE NO. 53

July 2, 1930, Wednesday, 8:45 p.m.

The meeting of July 2 represented the last time that Klanswoman Myrtle Hansen would be asked to fill in as temporary secretary. Few women within the order could match Myrtle's dedication to the Klavern, as she maintained one of the highest attendance rates of all the Grey Eagles. Forty-eight-year-old Myrtle was one of the few members who could legitimately state that her parents had not been first-generation immigrants.

Born Myrtle Humes in 1882, she married a farmer and business owner named Willian Hansen.[259] As both a budding farmer and successful proprietor of the Chippewa Ice Company, William and Myrtle lived a comfortable middle-class life. Residing in a two-story farmhouse at 520 Bridgewater Avenue on the West Hill, Myrtle and William had three sons.[260] While Myrtle and William enjoyed sustained financial comfort, their personal lives were filled with heartbreak and tragedy when their infant son Clare passed away.[261]

A woman who immensely enjoyed socializing with fellow women of the city, Myrtle was an active participant in several social clubs. She served as a high-ranking officer in the Rebekah Lodge, the female complement to the men's Odd Fellows fraternity. Myrtle was also an active member of the Masonic women's auxiliary, known as the Order of the Eastern Star. Religiously speaking, both William and Myrtle were devout Protestants who regularly attended the First Methodist Church of Chippewa Falls.

On this evening, as Myrtle could step back from secretarial duties, Klanswoman Tess Trainer was being reinstalled as Excellent Commander. Replacing Tess as Klavern secretary was the forty-six-year-old Mary Clark. Both women would end up attending every remaining Klonklave for Klan no. 14. With attendance plummeting to only six, Excellent Commander Trainer made it a goal that their meetings should start promptly at 8:45 p.m. and should never exceed the ten o'clock hour.

The meeting notes are as follows:

- *…motion…carried…Trainer act in Excellent Commander's absence*
- *Several…correspondence read…*
- *Have a time to start meetings…start on time. Also close on time, no later than 10 o'clock*
- *…adjourn until July 16*
- *Members Present—6*
- *Tess Trainer—Excellent Commander (Pro Tem)*
- *Myrtle Hansen—Kligrapp (Pro Tem)*[262]

KLONKLAVE NO. 54

July 16, 1930, Wednesday 9:00 p.m.

Unlike in past years, the installation of officers ceremony was condensed significantly, and the minutes only reference the Excellent Commander and Kligrapp. Attendance improved to nine members, and Excellent Commander Trainer took the opportunity to implore the members to persuade their delinquent sisters to reinstate themselves. If they couldn't get more women to pay the monthly dues, the Klavern ran a real risk of not being able to operate.

One of the women who heard this message was Anna Borgman, who took this meeting as an opportunity to pay her dues for another quarter. Like Klanswoman Myrtle Hansen, Anna Borgman had been a regular attendee at most of the meetings since the club's inception. Over the years, she had assumed the roles of several officer positions and was likely filling whatever role was needed of her at any given time.

Born to a Danish father and a German mother in 1881, Anna Anderson married William Borgman, the son of two German immigrants. Anna and William Borgman raised one daughter on a rural farm in Eagle Point Township.[263] Although the census officially listed her occupation as "housewife," her victory in the women's "nail driving contest" at the Dairymen's Picnic suggests that she had experience with manual labor on the family's farm.[264]

In addition to his farming obligations, William Borgman also served as an elected Chippewa County supervisor and a committee chairman for the Eagle Point Township's rural public school.[265] Revealing a deep commitment to their daughter's education, both parents served on committees set-up by the Victory School Parent Teacher's Association.[266] This activism seemed to rub off, as Helen Borgman earned honor-roll distinctions when she eventually attended Chippewa Falls Senior High School.[267]

As for the Grey Eagles, they were in dire need of getting more members like Klanswoman Anna Borgman. Whether the Excellent Commander's plan of bring back delinquent members would be effective remained to be seen.

The meeting notes are as follows:

- *New password given…*
- *New Excellent Commander, Tess Trainer, installed*

- *...talk on getting old members to reinstate*
- *Members Present—9*
- *Tess Trainer—Excellent Commander*
- *Mary Clark—Kligrapp*[268]

Klonklave No. 55

September 24, 1930, Wednesday, 8:30 p.m.

The Wisconsin Realm of the WKKK held its third-annual statewide convention during the last week in June, though the Grey Eagles did not give any specific acknowledgment in the minutes. In usual WKKK style, no mention appeared in any of the print media outlets in Wisconsin. The convention was hosted by the women of the WKKK's Walworth Klan no. 10, who operated within the Odd Fellows building in the city of Delavan.

What came out of the WKKK's third-annual Klorero was a list of seven resolutions that each Klan was expected to approve or reject. The resolutions were broken down into two categories. The first category were resolutions created by the delegates in attendance at the state convention. These include:

1. *Resolved...extend to Walworth Klan No. 10...appreciation...in entertaining said Klorero*
2. *Resolved...send greetings...Imperial Commander, Robbie Gill-Comer*
3. *Resolved...extend appreciation to Imperial Representative, Edith M. Hunt*
4. *Resolved...send Mary Jane Bishop...joy in learning that she is again able to engage in active service in our order*
5. *Resolved...go on record favoring the creation of greater active interest... welfare of our public schools*
6. *Resolved...endorse the 7th Resolution...to increase interest in state and local political affairs and...create a committee for that purpose*
7. *Resolved...pledge loyal support to help further the propagation of this state...a fund of $1,000.00...be created*

Of the seven resolutions adopted by the statewide convention, the Grey Eagles approved the first five but rejected the final two. For reasons not clarified, Klan no. 14 was not comfortable creating its own committee for increasing "interest in the Klan's state and local political affairs." The Grey Eagles also voted against the request that each unit help to finance a "fund of $1,000.00 for that purpose." A combination of factors likely weighed on their minds, including their own challenges of lackluster meeting attendance and growing financial concerns.

It is also possible that the women may have felt uneasy about the roles and activities that might be envisioned for these local committees. Would they be expected to trade away their anonymity and make themselves more politically visible? Losing the privacy and secrecy could risk exposure to political, social or economic boycotts at the hands of local Catholics. While national and state Klan leaders were used to being in the public sphere, the rank-and-file members certainly were not.

In addition to the seven proposals reached by the statewide delegates, a second batch of resolutions were produced by special state convention delegates on the "Good of the Order Committee":

1. *Resolved...Excellent Commanders instruct their Klanswomen to keep the inner affairs of the Klan strictly to themselves.*
2. *Resolved...Klanswomen wear their robes at all Klan meetings and remember their oath to "keep it spotless."*
3. *Resolved...send $2.00 a month towards expenses of Imperial Representative.*
4. *Resolved...obligation be given in Klonklave more often.*
5. *Resolved...work harder to get more reinstatements and get new members.*
6. *Resolved...have a school of instruction at province and state meetings.*

This second batch of resolutions was mostly dedicated to the expansion of the individual units, with special emphasis paid to the improvement and presentation of the regalia and ritual. The site of an individual dressed in a white Klan robe could produce a wide array of reactions ranging from curiosity and intrigue to hatred and fear, but the members were concerned because the choice of color made it extremely difficult to keep clean.

But it wasn't just the aesthetics of the robes that were getting lax. With low membership numbers plaguing most of the WKKK units, the rituals—most commonly the opening and closing ceremonies—were either carried out poorly, modified to be shorter or skipped altogether. As a result, one of the resolutions called for all state and provincial meetings to host a "school of instruction," where delegates could observe WKKK experts perform the rituals properly and then communicate what they learned to the members of their respective Klaverns. Above all else, however, was the desire to bring in more women.[269]

Of the thirteen total resolutions produced by the Klorero, the Grey Eagles approved eleven. After months of putting off the official vote, they also approved all eight of the Ellsworth Resolutions from the provincial convention in May.

The meeting notes are as follows:

- *…Delavan Resolutions…vetoed…6 and 7*
- *Resolved…adopt resolutions of Ellsworth*
- *Voted…$15.00 rent to Badger Club*
- *Members Present—5*
- *Tess Trainer—Excellent Commander*
- *Mary Clark—Kligrapp*[270]

Klonklave No. 56

November 19, 1930, Wednesday, 8:30 p.m.

Though the Grey Eagles had committed to holding a meeting on December 3, the November 19 Klonklave ended up being their final official gathering of the year. During this meeting, they authorized a rental payment to the Badger Club for the ongoing operational costs of the Hallie Klan Hall.

In fulfilling their obligation to one of the recently approved Delavan Resolutions, the Klanswomen voted to authorize a four-dollar payment to Imperial Representative Edith M. Hunt in Beloit for "office expenses." All layers of the WKKK were facing monetary challenges, as the Wisconsin Realm became more dependent on donations from its Klan units.

In a letter by Imperial Commander Robbie Gill-Comer to every women's unit in the country, it was revealed that the national WKKK had become increasingly concerned about financial negligence and potential theft and fraud in individual Klans. She wrote, "In the recent past we have suffered financial losses on account of a procedure which has been followed in some of the Klan units." Gill-Comer went on to explain how many Klaverns had placed just one Klanswoman in charge of the unit's money, which was in violation of the WKKK's constitution. She educated the women on the proper protocol and procedures associated with monetary collections.[271]

At least on paper, the various secretaries of the Grey Eagles appeared to be following the correct protocol. During each Klonklave, the secretary documented the money received in the meeting minutes and in a ledger known as the Kligrapp's Cash Book. Unfortunately, the Klan files do not contain specific documents pertaining to the role of a treasurer. In all likelihood, the lack of a consistently active membership made it difficult to properly fill the positions of the secretary and treasurer, which forced officers to juggle the responsibilities of multiple positions. Gill-Comer's fear was that these types of oversights and shortcuts could ultimately tempt a member to falsify records and engage in embezzlement. As a result, the Imperial Commander reminded the women that money withdrawn from their bank accounts can only happen when the check is signed by both the treasurer and the secretary.[272]

It wasn't just the misdeeds of a rogue member that could threaten the organization's finances but also the banks themselves. With the rapid closure of banks since the stock market crash, entire Klan units ran the risk of going bankrupt. In an official decree by the Wisconsin Realm Commander and Imperial Representative Edith Hunt, the WKKK ordered that each unit consolidate its financial holdings into one trusted bank account that would be kept in the bank under the name of just one trusted Klanswoman. The specific details regarding both of Klanswoman Hunt's orders were to be decided on and carried out by each individual unit.[273]

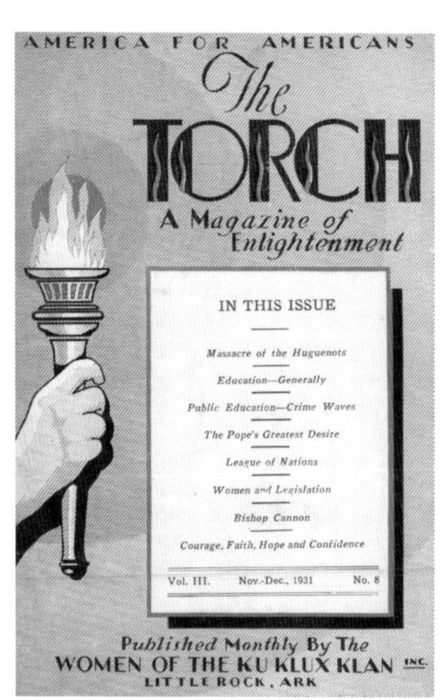

The WKKK's magazine was called *Torch: A Magazine of Enlightenment*, circa 1931. *Author's collection.*

Even if Klan no. 14 had not been following the WKKK's constitutional provisions to the letter, no evidence suggests that it had any problems with the misuse of club funds. Its records had been well documented and transparent to members. In any event, Klan no. 14's last major decision of the year was to allow the Klavern's treasurer to "draw all money and deposit [it] in a better way." The women were clearly worried about how they arranged their treasury and were eager for guidance to correct the issue. Meanwhile, a *Milwaukee Journal* editorial claimed that the Ku Klux Klan's nearly nine-million-membership peak in 1925 had plummeted to just more than thirty-four thousand in 1930.[274]

In a sign that the local Klans were attempting to preserve their order through consolidation, a social club announcement in the *Chippewa Herald* reported that members of the Badger Club had gathered at the Lafayette Township home of Klanswoman Mae Connell for a Bunco party. Thirty members were present from Eau Claire, Chippewa Falls, and Eagle Point, with an "elaborate lunch served at midnight."[275]

The meeting notes are as follows:

- *Motion…pay $15.00 rent to Badger Club, carried*
- *Voted…Klabee draw all money and deposit in a better way…*
- *Members Present—8*
- *Tess Trainer—Excellent Commander*
- *Mary Clark—Kligrapp*[276]

5

1931

Klonklave No. 57

February 20, 1931, Wednesday, 2:30 p.m.

With only six Klanswomen in attendance for the first meeting of the year, the membership challenges that carried over from 1930 were on full display. The women approached the new year with optimism, as they placed an order for a new dues book. Deciding to purchase the Wisconsin Realm's monthly newsletter only through the remainder of the month, however, revealed the stark reality

The women discussed various articles that had been published in the WKKK's monthly magazine. For an annual subscription cost of one dollar, it served as a primary communication device for Imperial Commander Robbie Gill-Comer. Each issue followed a similar format, including a greeting from the Imperial Commander, an assortment of member-submitted letters and stories and a "Klan Active" section, featuring updates from units around the country. Frequently reappearing topics were the support for public schools, opposition to the Catholic Church and the ongoing advocacy for prohibition.

Although no reason was provided, the minutes reveal the scheduling of a special Klonklave in just five days.

The meeting notes are as follows:

- *Voted...pay bulletins up to March 1st*
- *Wrote order...new dues book*

Left: A Grey Eagle visits a Civil War monument during a Klan gathering in Gettysburg, Pennsylvania, circa 1929. *Author's collection.*

Right: Daughter (Bernice Lekvin) and mother (Myra Ayers) twenty-five years after the dissolution of the Grey Eagles. *Private collection.*

- *Talk about "Torch Magazine"*
- *Next meeting…February 25th (evening)*
- *Members Present—6*
- *Tess Trainer—Excellent Commander*
- *Mary Clark—Kligrapp*[277]

Klonklave No. 58 (Special)

February 25, 1931, Wednesday, 8:30 p.m.

The last meeting of the Grey Eagles was labeled a special Klonklave. Six Klanswomen were in attendance—Myrtle Hansen, Cora Darbe, Emma

Dittmar, Mary Clark, Nettie Bollom and Tess Trainer—and Trainer initiated the meeting by discussing content within the WKKK's *Torch Magazine*. The most important development of the evening was the major modifications of future meetings. It had been decided that the Klan's next meeting would take place in the home of Klanswoman Myrtle Hansen instead of the Hallie Klan Hall. They also agreed that the meeting should take place earlier in the day and curiously left the gathering time vague. With little else to discuss, the Grey Eagles of the Chippewa Falls Women of the Ku Klux Klan, Klan no. 14, adjourned for the final time.

- *Discussion…"Torch Magazine"*
- *Talked about meeting in afternoon. Decided to hold next meeting with Hansen on the 4th of March…start no later than 2 o'clock*
- *6 members present: Klanswomen Hansen, Darbe, Dittmar, Clark, Bollom, and Trainer*
- *Motion…adjourn*
- *Members Present—6*
- *Tess Trainer—Excellent Commander*
- *Mary Clark—Kligrapp*[278]

AFTERWORD

By the spring of 1931, just more than seven years after the first cross burning in Chippewa Falls, formal Klan activity had ceased. The reasoning for the demise of the Grey Eagles cannot be neatly pinpointed, as a variety of local and national forces made an affiliation with the Klan toxic.

Maintaining a presence in Lake Hallie had become costly, and pressure to fund and operate the tabernacle escalated. Endless cycles of "member-funded" box socials had chased away many of the casual and cash-conscience members, as the group became more concerned with profits than Klan fellowship. Meanwhile, the stock market crash and the Great Depression made the for-profit picnics and quarterly dues payments seem like unaffordable luxuries. As financial concerns mounted, the Grey Eagles leadership saw their frustration rise toward the other women. Resentment festered.

Socially, the status of a Klan membership fell sharply. In 1924, wearing the robe exuded excitable intrigue from both supporters and detractors. By 1931, the Grey Eagles were displaying an unwillingness to don the robes. The recurring negative press had rightfully taken its toll on the national men's Klan's reputation. Although no documented acts of violence took place in the Chippewa Falls area, covert actions, such as bullying, discrimination, intimidation and mental and emotional abuse were likely present. It's possible that Klan members' reputations suffered in other social and fraternal circles as a result.

The Grey Eagles' political legacy is also murky, as many of their efforts centered on national politics rather than local. In 1924, the national government enacted two sweeping immigration laws, including the Labor Appropriations Act and the Johnson-Reed Act. The first established the United States Border Patrol, a federal agency tasked with combating smuggling and illegal immigration. The second, known as the Immigration Act of 1924, reduced the total number of immigrants allowed into the United States from 350,000 to 165,000 and enacted a quota system that purposely limited immigration from eastern and southern Europe.[1] In part to preserve these changes, the Grey Eagles sought to defeat Al Smith's candidacy for president in 1928. Fervor for and participation in that election was the most significant, overt political achievement of Klan no. 14.

Overall, it was the constitutional form of the United States government that ultimately undermined the Klan's presence in western Wisconsin. Those targeted by the Klan used the system to defend themselves. For example, Chippewa Falls passed a no-mask law, which was strictly enforced by the city's Catholic police chief. Robed Klansmen often preferred to drive around the city rather than lose their anonymity. In Cornell, Catholic priest Peter Minwegen jotted down license plate numbers of cars used in public parades and approached the owners after the fact. This led to awkward exchanges where businessmen were forced to choose between Klan ideology and the loss of Catholic customers. In some cases, known Klansmen were fired from their jobs, including a verbally abusive foreman at the Cornell Mill. Minwegen even purchased a piece of property in downtown Cornell where the Klan had burned a cross and constructed a new Catholic church there.[2] In Lake Hallie, one Catholic teenager interrupted a Klan night rally by starting a fire in dried corn stalks. The boy giggled with glee as the robed men frantically tried to put out the fire. Catholics, like the Klan, organized using the ballot box and earned much-needed political victories in local and countywide races.[3]

Unfortunately, many unanswered questions regarding the Grey Eagles remain. Did they engage in systemic "poison squad" behavior by undermining others through gossip, rumor and innuendo? How was the issue of race discussed within their Klavern, as there was no formal mention of race in four years of detailed meeting minutes? Did the women feel they improved their social standing in the eyes of their husbands, as the evidence suggests that it likely had?

As other Klan historians have uncovered, the Grey Eagles teetered on the edge of a historically anomalous strain of feminism, originating from the extreme right-wing flank of the U.S. political and cultural spectrum. They sought to validate a woman's right to vote by participating in causes championed by their husbands while carefully advancing their own position to improve conditions within Protestant homes. The women of Klan no. 14 successfully operated a sovereign Klavern, were invested as near-equal stakeholders in a tabernacle and raised awareness to issues such as alcohol abuse and the education of children. As members of a secret society, however, their impact was largely confined to their immediate circle of Protestant friends. To call them feminists would not be accurate, as they were mostly concerned with receiving a positive response from men rather than systemic improvements that challenged the structure controlled by men.

In the end, much of the Grey Eagles' platform did not come to fruition. Prohibition was repealed in 1933, racial eugenics fell out of favor after World War II and Roman Catholics failed to materialize as the internal national security threat the Klan predicted.

Today, most of the Lake Hallie locations connected to the Grey Eagles have been commercially developed as the area's population has grown. The cross-burning hill known as Round Top, the second hill east of U.S. Highway 53, is now home to a large municipal water tank and a communications tower. The primary farm field known as Klan Field, which had been ground zero for most of the Klan's rallies, now hosts retail and commercial properties, including the Walmart Supercenter.

The Klan's cherished Lake Hallie tabernacle had quite the journey prior to its destruction. Immediately following its Klan use, the building was turned into a notorious roadhouse known as the Midway. On Monday, June 15, 1931, federal Prohibition agents raided the property and arrested the new owner for "sale and possession of intoxicating liquors" to more than three hundred patrons. The newspaper reported that dry agents had been "unusually active" in the area, and federal agents announced that they were aware that the building had been used as a KKK tabernacle. It was likely the former Klan members themselves who called in the tip, as they were undoubtedly incensed that their Klavern had become a speakeasy.[4] Over the years, the building saw dance clubs, a bowling alley and supper club restaurants (Anchor Inn and Pier 53). On a Saturday in September 1993, the building was intentionally incinerated as part of a training exercise for the Lake Hallie Fire Department. A Holiday Gas Station and Burger King were later built on the site.[5]

As for the Grey Eagles, membership card stubs indicate that a total of forty-two women had paid at least one quarterly membership between

Left: The Lake Hallie Klan Tabernacle went through several owners and aesthetic changes, including a cabaret, bowling alley and restaurants. In 1993, it was razed during firefighter training. *Leader Telegram.*

Below: The Hallie Hills today, including Dana's Bluff (*left*) and Round Top (*right*). Once used for cross-burnings, Round Top is now home to a municipal water tower. *Photo by Savannah Skora.*

1927 and 1931, although no more than thirty-one paid their dues simultaneously. The average age of the group in 1928 was 41.6. The oldest member was 68-year-old Dora Strong, while the youngest was 21-year-old Agnes Butler. Half of the women had at least one parent born in a foreign country, and nearly all were devout Protestants, particularly Methodist and Lutheran. Economically, their husbands maintained middle-class occupations, including jeweler, grocer, teacher, mechanic, train car inspector, postal carrier, mill foreman, painter, carpenter, salesman,

The site of the Klan's Tabernacle in Lake Hallie is now home to a gas station and fast food restaurant complex. *Photo by Savannah Skora.*

shipping clerk, furniture repairman, railroad telegraph operator and general laborer. A disproportionate number of the men, fifteen in total, were self-employed farmers. It's possible that farmers and railroad workers feared the competition from immigrants more and worried less about being economically boycotted by Catholics. A few of the Grey Eagles would go on to serve as nurse, teacher, seamstress or waitress, but the vast majority lived as empowered matriarchal homemakers.

By the late 1930s, the WKKK was no more. Robbie Gill-Comer, the once dominant Imperial Commander and prominent icon for conservative Protestant women, lived out her remaining years in Los Angeles, where she died of a heart attack in 1963 at the age of eighty.[6] She lived long enough to see the election of John F. Kennedy as the first Catholic president of the United States. The WKKK's Imperial Representative for the Realm of Wisconsin, Mary Bishop, left the WKKK and became a journalist in Grand Rapids, Michigan. In 1946, she succumbed to uterine cancer at fifty-three,[7] and the WKKK's Wisconsin Realm Commander, Edith M. Hunt, died in Janesville, Wisconsin, in 1974.

The controversial Pat Malone left the Klan and started his own traveling ministry. Advertising himself as an "internationally known evangelist," Malone gave sermons on the "Greatness of God," which included a "black widow spider, sea horses, rattle snake fangs, a baby octopus, and other curiosities."[8] His sermon on "A Little Bit of Heaven" featured a "half-ton structure of dull rocks" that stood "nine feet high and twelve feet wide." Once light was shown on the rocks, "they would appear fluorescent" and "illuminate a darkened auditorium." Malone died on Valentine's Day in 1963.[9]

As for the post-Klan activism of Tess Trainer and Nettie Bollom, the two women who served as Excellent Commanders of the Grey Eagles, they immediately expanded their roles within the Chippewa Falls chapter of the Women's Christian Temperance Union. Each held constitutional offices in the organization and hosted club meetings in their homes. Their activism with the WCTU lasted until 1936, three years after Prohibition was officially repealed at the national level.[10]

Aside from their efforts in the WCTU, Nettie and Tess forged diverging life paths in the remaining years of their lives. Nettie continued operation of the family jewelry store in downtown Chippewa Falls and witnessed her children assist in the founding of a new community church, Christian Gospel Chapel, in the parlor of her living room. The inaugural sermons given by the pastor were "Worshipping God" and "Seeking the Lost."[11] Throughout the 1930s and '40s, the church became locally known for its extensive global missionary works, including assisting poor villagers in places like Nyasaland, Africa, and Bolivia, South America. Nettie was a frequent volunteer in the church and was known for her poem readings, recitations and volunteerism in the kitchen. She was known by those around her as a "god-fearing, fair-minded, no-nonsense," yet "loving and kind soul" who treated "everyone with dignity and respect." After conducting twenty-three interviews with those who knew her, all appeared to be in genuine disbelief regarding her participation in the Klan, though they did acknowledge her disapproval of alcohol. Nettie passed away in 1972 at the age of eighty-six and was buried in the family plot in Osseo, Wisconsin.[12]

Tess Trainer's crusade against alcohol peaked during the 1932 presidential election. In a letter to the editor, Trainer implored women to unite against candidate Franklin Roosevelt as they had against Al Smith in 1928. She warned that a Roosevelt administration would lobby both Congress and individual state governments to repeal the Eighteenth Amendment. Tess concluded her letter with a poem:

The Things That Matter
Not what we have, but what we use,
Not what we see, but what we choose,
These are the things that mar or bless,
The sum of human happiness.

Not what we take, but what we give,
Not as we pray, but as we live;
These are the things that make for peace,
Both now and after time shall cease.[13]

Roosevelt went on to beat President Hoover, as economic fears trumped other issues. Trainer's final years were spent in relative seclusion in the heart of logging country in northern Wisconsin because her husband had been assigned railroad station manager in the town of Fifield. While residents remember seeing Frank Trainer at the station, none could recall Tess. As one ninety-seven-year-old resident quipped, "If the woman disliked drinkin' she probably hated Fifield."[14] On the morning of May 1, 1947, Tess died of a cerebral hemorrhage at her home. Her body was interred at Fifield cemetery, and her husband joined her in 1956.[15] Tess's only son, Boyd Bidwell, lived to be eighty-five-years-old and resided in New Orleans, Louisiana. His life ended in 1986, after being struck by a motorist while walking home.

The overwhelming majority of the Grey Eagles lived long enough to see society change in ways they could not have imagined in the late 1920s, including the rise and fall of Nazism, the atomic bomb, the Cold War, modern feminism and the civil rights movement. With all of the original Grey Eagles now deceased, what remains are the observations, reflections and testimonials of surviving grandchildren. Out of twenty-seven interviews I conducted with relatives, common initial responses emerged, including general shock, disbelief, confusion, concern over the family name and, in one case, denial. While a few were able to acknowledge family rumors of their grandfather possibly participating, the overwhelming majority were dumbfounded by the shear notion of their grandmother having been a member.

Each relative had good reason to question their grandmother's Klan associations, as more than four-fifths of the families I interviewed were now religiously and/or racially diverse. A handful of grandchildren were shocked by the anti-Catholic connection because they could vividly recall their grandmother's adoration, and in some cases support, for Kennedy. As

Tess Trainer's grave in Fifield, Wisconsin, located some one hundred miles northeast of Chippewa Falls. *Photo by John Kinville.*

I carefully walked through the evidence with each surviving relative, more commonalities emerged, including their grandmother's caution toward alcohol and deep commitment to the Christian faith.[16] The most notable constant was that their grandmothers had kept their past Klan affiliation a carefully guarded secret. Who could blame them? As the male-only Klan evolved in the 1940s and 1970s, many units openly embraced Hitlerism and were purposely inseparable from the American neo-Nazi movement.

While it's irresponsible to assume that all, or event most, of the Grey Eagles evolved completely away from their Klan ideologies, the lives that they lived in front of their children and grandchildren indicate that they had grown with the changing times. It's possible that this growth began during the Klan years, which might explain why Trainer and Bollom had such difficulty getting women to attend meetings and pay dues.

The Great Depression and World War II weren't simply passive historical events but also life-encompassing moments that physically happened to people. Perhaps these events helped shape a different worldview for many of these women. What is known for certain is that the Grey Eagles left the WKKK voluntarily, as did the members from every other Wisconsin Klan unit in the early 1930s. By the time each of the Grey Eagles had grandchildren, each was largely viewed as a strong matriarch who believed in "setting a good example," "minding what you say and do to others," "striving for honesty and integrity" and "learning from your past mistakes."[17] In addition to raising their children and grandchildren, nearly all of the women remained active in their churches and other social and fraternal affiliations. In the end, they seemed to go on to model a much different worldview than what their earlier selves envisioned for the country.

Today, most of the Grey Eagles are buried near one another at either Prairie View Cemetery in Lake Hallie or Forest Hill Cemetery in Chippewa Falls. Death serves all of us a reminder that the tribal differences we think we hold dear are often fleeting. The Chippewa Falls area is a better place to live despite the efforts of the Grey Eagles but also because of them. Our area was once given starkly divergent choices on how we should live and interact with one another as a community. The larger society chose tolerance and empathy. The post-Klan lives of the Grey Eagles, including the lifelong secrecy of their membership and the purposeful modeling of positive social values to their grandchildren, leave us with a tacit admission that they had indeed gotten it wrong. The women were certainly a product of their generation in the 1920s and 1930s, but they also successfully became a product of future generations as well.

APPENDIX

1928 Officer List

Excellent Commander (President)	Tess Trainer
Klaliff (Vice President)	Agnes Clark
Klokard (Lecturer)	Mae Connell
Kludd (Chaplain)	Nettie Bollom
Kligrapp (Secretary)	Bernice Lekvin
Klabee (Treasurer)	Olga Smock
Kladd (Conductor)	Clara Lange
Klarogo (Inner Guard)	Grace Fisher
Klexter (Outer Guard)	Ruth Peterson
Klokan Chief (Advisor/Investigator)	Mary Clark
Klokan No. 1 (Advisor/Investigator)	Eleanor Kopischkie
Klokan No. 2 (Advisor/Investigator)	Dora Strong
Kourier No. 1 (For rituals)	Anna Borgman
Kourier No. 2 (For rituals)	Henrietta Tracy
Night Hawk (For rituals)	Emma Hoover
Musicklad (Pianist)	Grace Tracy

COMPREHENSIVE GREY EAGLES MEMBERSHIP LIST

(Paid at least one quarterly dues payment of $1.50)

Member Tally	Last Name (Maiden Name)	First Name	Life Span	Age in 1928	Age at Death
1	Arnold (Hudson)	Eva	1893–1976	35	83
2	Ayers	Myra	1879–1962	49	83
3	Bollom (Larson)	Nettie	1885–1972	43	86
4	Borgman (Anderson)	Anna	1881–1960	47	79
5	Butler (Clark)	Agnes	1907–2003	21	96
6	Butler	Della	1866–1937	62	71
7	Buttenhoff	Emma	1895–1969	33	74
8	Campbell	Flora	1885–1936	43	51
9	Card (Sloan)	Mary	1878–1953	50	74
10	Clark	Mary	1884–1970	44	86
11	Clem (Copper)	Lillie	1887–1944	41	57
12	Connell	Mae	1886–1954	42	67
13	Darbe	Cora	1871–1943	57	72
14	Dittmar (Happle)	Emma	1868–1951	60	83
15	Earl (Dana)	Eva	1878–1939	50	61
16	Ellsworth	Adella	1877–1960	51	82
17	Fisher (Fritzinger)	Grace	1880–1981	48	101
18	Hansen (Humes)	Myrtle	1883–1964	45	81
19	Hempelman (Cameron)	Mary	1888–1980	40	91
20	Hoover (Hanson)	Emma	1904–1939	24	35
21	Klages (Klemke)	Emma	1884–1960	44	75
22	Kopischkie (McDonald)	Eleanor	1891–1981	37	90
23	Kurth	Minnie	1895–1986	33	91

Member Tally	Last Name (Maiden Name)	First Name	Life Span	Age in 1928	Age at Death
24	Lange (Gamper)	Clara	1891–1963	37	71
25	Lekvin (Ayers)	Bernice	1904–1990	24	85
26	Mason	Ella	1875–1952	53	77
27	Nelson (Love)	Belle	1877–1958	51	81
28	Nihart (Sippel)	Emma	1889–1966	39	76
29	Olsen (Tracy)	Grace	1902–1981	26	79
30	Peterson	Mildred	1902–1970	26	68
31	Peterson (Modine)	Ruth	1898–1980	30	82
32	Popple (Richardson)	Floretta	1900–1990	28	90
33	Rude (Moen)	Anna	1887–1974	41	86
34	Shaffer	Emma	1885–1963	43	78
35	Smock (Weitherick)	Olga	1873–1949	55	76
36	Strong (Butler)	Dora	1860–1957	68	97
37	Swan (Parker)	Lettie	1886–1958	42	72
38	Tracy (Castleton)	Henrietta (Etta)	1870–1942	58	72
39	Trainer (Eley)	Tessie (Tess)	1881–1947	47	65
40	Wallace	Josie	Unknown		
41	Waller (Berntson)	Hannah	1883–1927	44	44
42	Waller (Parker)	Laurel	1889–1947	39	58

NOTES

Introduction

1. David Mark Chalmers, *Hooded Americanism: The History of the Ku Klux Klan* (Durham, NC: Duke University Press, 2007).
2. Kathleen M. Blee, *Women of the Klan: Racism and Gender in the 1920s* (Berkeley: University of California Press, 2009), 1–3.
3. Ibid., 7.
4. Ibid., 123–53.
5. Ibid., 3.
6. Craig Fox, *Everyday Klansfolk: White Protestant Life and the KKK in 1920s Michigan* (East Lansing: Michigan State University Press, 2011).
7. Blee, *Women of the Klan*.
8. Laura Smith, "The KKK Started a Branch Just for Women in the 1920s, and Half a Million Joined," Medium, Timeline, June 28, 2017, https://timeline.com.
9. Blee, *Women of the Klan*, 3.

Part I

Chapter 1

1. Chalmers, *Hooded Americanism*, 8–9.
2. "Ku Klux Act Passed by Congress," History, A&E Television Networks, February 09, 2010, https://www.history.com.

3. Chalmers, *Hooded Americanism*, 20–21.
4. Ibid, 8–9.
5. Ibid, 16–25.

Chapter 2

6. Chalmers, *Hooded Americanism*, 26–27.
7. Alexis Clark, "How 'The Birth of a Nation' Revived the Ku Klux Klan," History, A&E Television Networks, August 14, 2018, https://www.history.com.
8. Ibid.
9. "Birth of a Nation," *Chippewa Herald*, November 21, 1915.
10. "Klan Is Established with Impressiveness," *Atlanta Constitution*, November 28, 1915.
11. Norman Fredric Weaver, "The Knights of the Ku Klux Klan in Wisconsin, Indiana, Ohio and Michigan" (PhD diss., University of Wisconsin–Madison, 1954).
12. Paul D Ostwald, "The Activities of the Ku Klux Klan in Chippewa County During the 1920s" (master's thesis, University of Wisconsin–Eau Claire, 1970).
13. "Special KKK Bulletin," October 18, 1926.

Chapter 3

14. *Ideals of the Women the Ku Klux Klan* (Little Rock, AR: Imperial Headquarters Women of the Ku Klux Klan, 1923).
15. *Women of America!: The Past! The Present! The Future!: Outline of Principles and Teachings*. (Little Rock, AR: Imperial Headquarters Women of the Ku Klux Klan, 1923).
16. History.com editors, "Eugenics," History, A&E Television Networks, November 15, 2017. https://www.history.com.
17. *Ideals of the Women the Ku Klux Klan*.
18. Thomas R. Pegram, *One Hundred Percent American: The Rebirth and Decline of the Ku Klux Klan in the 1920s* (Chicago: Ivan R, 2011).
19. 14th Census of Population, *1920* (Washington, D.C.: National Archives and Records Administration, 1993).
20. Ibid.

21. Ostwald, "Activities of the Ku Klux Klan."
22. *Attitude of the Knights of the Ku Klux Klan Toward the Roman Catholic Hierarchy* (Atlanta, GA: Imperial Headquarters of the Ku Klux Klan, 1923).
23 *The Public School Problem in America* (Atlanta, GA: Imperial Headquarters of the Ku Klux Klan, 1923).

Chapter 4

24. "Efforts to Organize a Klan Being Made," *Eau Claire Leader*, January 30, 1924.
25. "Fiery Cross Burns on Chippewa Hill," *Chippewa Herald*, February 11, 1924.
26. "Another Fiery Cross on Hill Arouses City Sunday," *Chippewa Herald*, February 18, 1924.
27. "Special KKK Bulletin," October 18, 1926.
28. Minwegen, Peter, OMI, "Reminiscences," University of Wisconsin, 1972, http://digital.library.wisc.edu.
29. *14th Census of Population, 1920*.
30. "18,000 Gather at Klan Meeting at Cornell," *Eau Claire Leader*, July 12, 1924.
31. "Thousands Crowd Cornell to View Klansmen Parade," *Chippewa Herald*, July 12, 1924.

Chapter 5

32. Blee, *Women of the Klan*, 24–27.
33. Ibid., 26.
34. *Constitution and Laws of the Women of the Ku Klux Klan* (Little Rock, AR: Imperial Headquarters Women of the Ku Klux Klan, 1923).
35. *American Women* (Little Rock, AR: Imperial Headquarters of the Women's Ku Klux Klan, 1924).
36. *The Equality of Woman: Women of the Ku Klux Klan* (Little Rock, AR: Imperial Headquarters Women of the Ku Klux Klan, 1923).
37. "Business Meeting," *Chippewa Herald*, August 26, 1924.
38. Miscellaneous 1926–30, Women of the Ku Klux Klan, Chippewa Falls, University of Wisconsin Digital Collections, 1.
39. Ibid.

40. Ibid.
41. "Klan Leader Is Re-Elected at Biennial Meet," *Eau Claire Leader*, September 15, 1926.
42. Quarterly Reports, 1926–30, Women of the Ku Klux Klan, Chippewa Falls, University of Wisconsin Digital Collections.
43. Miscellaneous 1926–30, Women of the Ku Klux Klan, 2.
44. *New Encyclopedia of Southern Culture*, vol. 24, *Race*, Thomas C. Holt and Laurie B. Green, eds. (Chapel Hill: University of North Carolina Press, 2013), 234.
45. Miscellaneous 1926–30, Women of the Ku Klux Klan, 2.
46. Ibid.

PART II

Chapter 1

1. "Expect Thousands at Gathering of Ku Klux Klan: Elaborate Program Planned for Meeting Hooded Order to Be Held at Fairgrounds," *Oshkosh Northwestern*, July 29, 1927.
2. "Voters' Apathy Draws Fire of Klan Leader," *Eau Claire Leader*, August 3, 1927.
3. "Leaders of Klan Claim National Crisis Is at Hand," *Oshkosh Northwestern*, August 1, 1927.
4. Ibid.
5. "Voters' Apathy Draws Fire," *Eau Claire Leader*.
6. Mark Jones, "The Klan Leaves Its Mark on Washington's Airwaves," *Boundary Stones* (blog), WETA, January 13, 2005, https://blogs.weta.org.
7. "Muffling the Klan," *Eau Claire Leader*, July 2, 1927.
8. Fox, *Everyday Klansfolk*.
9. United States Census Bureau, *1930* United States Census—Wisconsin, Chippewa County, Wheaton, District 0030, U.S. Department of Commerce, www.ancestry.com.
10. "Notes from Our Neighbors," *Argos Reflector*, December 20, 1906.
11. Indiana, Marriages, *1810–2001*, Ancestry.com.
12. United States Census Bureau. 1910, 1920, and 1930 United States Census—Indiana and Wisconsin, U.S. Department of Commerce, ancestry.com.
13. U.S. City Directories, 1822–1995, Ancestry.com.

14. "Ice Cream Social and Program," *Chippewa Herald*, July 15, 1927.
15. U.S. City Directories, 1822–1995, Ancestry.com.
16. U.S. Const. amend. XVIII, section 1.
17. Minutes of the Women of the Ku Klux Klan in Chippewa Falls, Wisconsin, 1927–1931, University of Wisconsin Digital Collections, no. 1.
18. "Four Sentenced in Flogging Case," *Eau Claire Leader*, August 9, 1927.
19. "Pat Malone Has Roast for Grand Dragon Hammond," *Eau Claire Leader*, August 19, 1927.
20. John A Turcheneske, "Ku Klux Klan in Northwestern Wisconsin" (master's thesis, University of Wisconsin–River Falls, 1971), 13–21.
21. "Pat Malone Pleads Guilty of Slander: Klan Lecturer to Expose Order, He Tells Senator Chase," *Wisconsin State Journal*, June 5, 1927.
22. "Two Demented Men Seek Protection; Declare They Are Chased by Klan," *Eau Claire Leader*, August 20, 1927.
23. Minutes, Women of the Ku Klux Klan in Chippewa Falls, no. 2.
24. "Mental Victim of Klan Had a Small Fortune," *Eau Claire Leader*, August 23, 1927.
25. Minutes, Women of the Ku Klux Klan in Chippewa Falls, no. 3.
26. Ibid.
27. Ibid.
28. Ibid.
29. "Voice of the People: Praise for John Sharp Williams," *Eau Claire Leader*, September 17, 1927.
30. Ibid.
31. "Pastor Denies He Abducted Successor," *Eau Claire Leader*, September 18, 1927.
32. "Knapp News Briefs," *Eau Claire Leader*, September 14, 1927.
33. *Kloran or Ritual of the Women of the Ku Klux Klan*, Women of the Ku Klux Klan, 1928.
34. Minutes, Women of the Ku Klux Klan in Chippewa Falls, no. 4.
35. "Chippewa Falls Obituaries: Hannah Waller," *Eau Claire Leader*, October 4, 1927.
36. *Funeral Services: Women of the Ku Klux Klan* (Little Rock, AR: Knights of the Ku Klux Klan, 1925); *Burial Service: Women of the Ku Klux Klan* (Little Rock, AR: Knights of the Ku Klux Klan, 1925).
37. "Chippewa Falls Obituaries: Hannah Waller," *Eau Claire Leader*, October 4, 1927.
38. *Constitution and Laws of the Women of the Ku Klux Klan* (Little Rock, AR: Pugh and Company, 1927), 1–73.

39. Ibid., 4.
40. Ibid., 4.
41. Minutes, Women of the Ku Klux Klan in Chippewa Falls, no. 5.
42. *Fish Pond Game Directions* (Springfield, MA: Milton Bradley Corporation, 1909).
43. Minutes, Women of the Ku Klux Klan in Chippewa Falls, no. 6.
44. "Supreme Court Affirms Ruling Against Unions—Injunctions Against United Mine Workers Held Legal—Large Pittsburgh Coal Company Announces Cut in Wage Rate," *Eau Claire Leader*, October 18, 1927.
45. Minutes, Women of the Ku Klux Klan in Chippewa Falls, no. 6.
46. Ibid., no. 7.
47. United States Census Bureau, 1930 United States Census—Wisconsin, Chippewa County, Hallie, District 0030, U.S. Department of Commerce, ancestry.com.
48. "Archives," Evangelical Lutheran Church in America," https://www.elca.org; "Swedish American Baptisms, Marriages, Deaths, and Burials," Immanuel Lutheran Church, ELCA Film Number M41, SSIRC Film Number: E-41, https://www.ancestry.com.
49. "Chippewa Falls Obituaries: Everett S. Parker," *Eau Claire Leader*, October 29, 1927.
50. Minutes, Women of the Ku Klux Klan in Chippewa Falls, no. 7.
51. "Woodward for Senate?," *Eau Claire Leader*, November 3, 1927.
52. "Another Coolidge Man in Senate Race," *Eau Claire Leader*, August 23, 1925.
53. "La Follette Scores the Ku Klux Klan; Asserts He Is Opposed to Any Discrimination Between Races, Classes and Creeds. Says It Cannot Survive He Insists, However, That the Great Issue Is Breaking of the Power of Private Monopoly," *New York Times*, August 23, 1924.
54. "Woodward Charges That Candidacy Is Buried by Press," *Eau Claire Leader*, September 10, 1925.
55. "Lafollette Sweeps All Before Him: Progressive Candidate for Senator Rolls Up a Majority," *Eau Claire Leader*, September 16, 1925.
56. "Lafollette Easy Victor in Senate Election," *Eau Claire Leader*, September 30, 1925.
57. Minutes, Women of the Ku Klux Klan in Chippewa Falls, no. 8.
58. "Merrill Herald Grows Pessimistic," *Eau Claire Leader*, November 17, 1927.
59. United States Census Bureau, 1920 United States Census—Wisconsin, Chippewa County, Eagle Point Township, U.S. Department of Commerce, ancestry.com.
60. Minutes, Women of the Ku Klux Klan in Chippewa Falls, no. 9.

61. "Home Unit of Nation Says Speaker: Women Urged to Take Interest in Community Life and Use Ballot," *Herald-Palladium*, March 27, 1919.
62. Minutes, Women of the Ku Klux Klan in Chippewa Falls, no.9.
63. 1930 United States Census Wisconsin, Chippewa County, Hallie, ancestry.com.
64. Minutes, Women of the Ku Klux Klan in Chippewa Falls, no. 10.
65. Ibid.
66. Ibid.

Chapter 2

67. "Governor Al Smith Refuses Probe Asked by Klan," *Eau Claire Leader*, December 31, 1927.
68. United States Census Bureau, 1940 United States Federal Census, U.S. Department of Commerce, ancestry.com.
69. "Obituaries—George A. Lange," *Chippewa Herald*, May 28, 1997; "Area Obituaries—Mrs. George Lange," *Eau Claire Leader*, November 19, 1963.
70. *Kloran or Ritual of the Women of the Ku Klux Klan*, Women of the Ku Klux Klan, 1928.
71. Ibid.
72. Minutes, Women of the Ku Klux Klan in Chippewa Falls, no. 11.
73. "Klansmen Will Discard Masks on February 22nd," *Eau Claire Leader*, January 22, 1928.
74. Ibid.
75. Alice Robb, "How Sunglasses Make You Less Generous," *New Republic*, March 26, 2014, www.newrepublic.com.
76. Minutes, Women of the Ku Klux Klan in Chippewa Falls, no. 12.
77. Ibid.
78. "Demurrer in Case Against Klan Denied," *Eau Claire Leader*, February 9, 1928.
79. United States Census Bureau, 1930 United States Federal Census, U.S. Department of Commerce, ancestry.com.
80. "Obituaries—Orrin Kurth," *Eau Claire Leader*, September 8, 1971.
81. Ibid.
82. *MusiKlan* (Little Rock, AR: Imperial Headquarters of the Women's Ku Klux Klan, 1928).
83. Ibid.
84. Ibid.

85. *The Twelfth Chapter of Romans as a Klansman's Law of Life* (Little Rock, AR: Imperial Headquarters of the Women's Ku Klux Klan, 1928).
86. Ibid.
87. Minutes, Women of the Ku Klux Klan in Chippewa Falls, no. 14.
88. *Oath of Allegiance—KKK and WKKK* (Little Rock, AR: Imperial Headquarters of the Women's Ku Klux Klan, 1928).
89. Ibid.
90. Ibid.
91. "Klan Getaway," *Oshkosh Northwestern*, March 2, 1928.
92. Ibid.
93. "Nice, Ladylike Order?," *Oshkosh Northwestern*, March 2, 1928.
94. "Ethel Mary Tilton—Teacher of Singing," *Eau Claire Leader*, February 3, 1928.
95. United States Census Bureau, 1920 United States Federal Census.
96. "Says Klan Seized Chippewa County Elections in '24," *Eau Claire Leader*, April 14, 1928.
97. "Tilton Held on State Health Board Charge," *Eau Claire Leader*, June 18, 1927.
98. "Tilton Is Fined $500," *Chippewa Herald*, June 18, 1928.
99. "Island's Donor Is Honored by City's Scout Troop 13," *Chippewa Herald*, February 20, 1963.
100. Minutes, Women of the Ku Klux Klan in Chippewa Falls, no. 15.
101. Ibid.
102. Ibid., no. 16.
103. "Women of the Klux Klux Klan," Longansport Ku Klux Klan Quartette, 1925.
104. United States Census Bureau, 1920 United States Federal Census.
105. "Earl Hempelman Dies at Ashland Hospital," *Chippewa Herald*, November 29, 1932.
106. Minutes, Women of the Ku Klux Klan in Chippewa Falls, no. 16.
107. *America for Americans—Creed of a Klanswoman* (Little Rock, AR: Women of the Ku Klux Klan, 1928).
108. "Mrs. Cora Darbe of Falls Passes Away on Sunday, *Sheboygan Press*, December 27, 1943.
109. United States Census Bureau, 1930 United States Federal Census.
110. Minutes, Women of the Ku Klux Klan in Chippewa Falls, no. 17.
111. "Voice of the People: E.E. Heyle Bets Thousand on Democrat," *Chippewa Herald*, April 1, 1928.
112. "Stephenson Unmasked in Prison Talk," *Chippewa Herald*, April 2, 1928.

113. "Witness at Pittsburgh Klan Case Testifies He Was Present at the Burning Alive of Several Victims," *Eau Claire Leader*, April 11, 1928.
114. "Klan Organizer Attacks Policy of Hiram Evans: W.J. Simmons, Former Leader, Files Deposition," *Chippewa Herald*, April 8, 1928.
115. "W.R.C. Elects Officers for Coming Year," *Chippewa Herald*, December 11, 1928.
116. "Woman's Relief Corps," 2017. http://womansreliefcorps.org.
117. United States Census Bureau, *1*930 United States Federal Census.
118. "Farmer Unions in Joint Meeting at Bloomer Friday," *Eau Claire Leader*, February 20, 1935.
119. "Tilden Mills Progressive Club Meets," *Eau Claire Leader*, April 13, 1934.
120. "Pythian Sisters Appoint Committees for Year," *Chippewa Herald*, January 25, 1939.
121. Minutes, Women of the Ku Klux Klan in Chippewa Falls, no. 18.
122. "Voice of the People: The Imperial Wizard of Ku Klux Klan Writes a Letter," *Eau Claire Leader*, April 21, 1928.
123. Minutes, Women of the Ku Klux Klan in Chippewa Falls, "Bulletin."
124. Ibid., no. 19.
125. "Presbyterian Missionary Circle to Meet Friday," *Chippewa Herald*, November 7, 1923.
126. Ibid.
127. United States Census Bureau, 1930 United States Federal Census.
128. "Jim Falls Items," *Chippewa Herald*, January 24, 1929.
129. "Mrs. Phillips Elected District President of the W.R.C.," *Chippewa Herald*, October 20, 1930.
130. "Testifies Klan Paid Heflin for Speeches Attacking Governor Smith," *Chippewa Herald*, June 1, 1928.
131. Minutes, Women of the Ku Klux Klan in Chippewa Falls, no. 20.
132. "Obituaries—Mrs. Mary Clark," *Chippewa Herald*, December 21, 1970.
133. "Obituaries—Agnes C. Butler," *Chippewa Herald*, April 14, 2003.
134. Minutes, Women of the Ku Klux Klan in Chippewa Falls, no. 21.
135. Robert Elliot Chiles, *The Revolution of '28: Al Smith, American Progressivism, and the Coming of the New Deal* (Ithaca, NY: Cornell University Press, 2018).
136. Robert K. Murray, *The 103rd Ballot: The Legendary 1924 Democratic Convention That Forever Changed Politics* (New York: HarperCollins, 2016).
137. United States Census Bureau, 1930 United States Federal Census.
138. *Constitution and Laws of the Women of the Ku Klux Klan.*
139. "Effatha Lutheran Church," *Chippewa Herald*, June 26, 1928.
140. Ibid.

141. Minutes, Women of the Ku Klux Klan in Chippewa Falls, no. 22.
142. "Klan Joke," *Eau Claire Leader*, July 11, 1928.
143. United States Census Bureau, 1900 United States Federal Census, U.S. Department of Commerce, ancestry.com.
144. United States Census Bureau, 1920 United States Federal Census.
145. "Obituary of Harvey Ayers," *Eau Claire Leader*, December 14, 1943.
146. *Installation Ceremonies: Women of the Ku Klux Klan* (Little Rock, AR: Imperial Headquarters of the Women's Ku Klux Klan, 1928).
147. Ibid.
148. Minutes, Women of the Ku Klux Klan in Chippewa Falls, no. 23.
149. Minutes, Women of the Ku Klux Klan in Chippewa Falls, "Attention!!! Patriot Americans—The *Fellowship Forum*."
150. "Backing of Klan Goal of G.O.P. Solon Is View," *Evening Sun*, January 29, 1930; "KNEA Favors Educational Bill," *Courier-Journal*, April 19, 1930.
151. Minutes, Women of the Ku Klux Klan in Chippewa Falls, "Province County List."
152. Minutes, Women of the Ku Klux Klan in Chippewa Falls, no. 24.
153. Fox, *Everyday Klansfolk*, 93, 190–91.
154. "Iron River, Michigan," *Eau Claire Leader*, August 25, 1928.
155. Robert A. Slayton, *Empire Statesman: The Rise and Redemption of Al Smith*. (New York: Free Press, 2001).
156. *Kloran*, Women of the Ku Klux Klan.
157. Minutes, Women of the Ku Klux Klan in Chippewa Falls, no. 25.
158. "D.C.O.P Building Initiated," *Eau Claire Leader*, August 1, 1928.
159. Minutes, Women of the Ku Klux Klan in Chippewa Falls, no. 26.
160. "Mrs. A.E. Clem, Chippewa, Dies," *Eau Claire Leader*, August 26, 1944.
161. "To Pay Respects," *Chippewa Herald*, August 25, 1944.
162. Letter from the Realm Office, March 28, 1930, University of Wisconsin Digital Collections,
163. Blee, *Women of the Klan*, 158–60.
164. Letter from the Realm Office, March 28, 1930.
165. Ibid.
166. Ibid.
167. Minutes, Women of the Ku Klux Klan in Chippewa Falls, no. 27.
168. Letter from the Bond Department, 1928, University of Wisconsin Digital Collections.
169. Minutes, Women of the Ku Klux Klan in Chippewa Falls, no. 28.
170. "Malone, Klan Case up in Supreme Court Monday," *Chippewa Herald*, September 30, 1928.

171. "Chippewa Falls Personals—Paul H. Raihle," *Chippewa Herald*, October 12, 1928.
172. "Letter to the Editor," *Eau Claire Leader*, October 7, 1928.
173. Minutes, Women of the Ku Klux Klan in Chippewa Falls, no. 29.
174. "Smith Attacks Anti-Saloon League and Klan In Address," *Eau Claire Leader*, October 30, 1928.
175. "Receivership Requested for Ku Klux Klan," *Eau Claire Leader*, October 16, 1928.
176. "Federal Court Asked to Name Receiver," *Atlanta Constitution*, October 16, 1928.
177. "Klan Joke," *Eau Claire Leader*, October 30, 1928.
178. "Man Found Near Death with Klan Brands on Body," *Eau Claire Leader*, November 2, 1928.
179. Minutes, Women of the Ku Klux Klan in Chippewa Falls, no. 30.
180. Marc Schulman, "1928 Election Results Hoover V. Smith," History Central, 2018, http://www.historycentral.com.
181. Leip David, "1928 Presidential General Election Results—Wisconsin," Atlas of U.S. Presidential Elections, 2016. www.uselectionatlas.org.
182. "Smith Victor in Chippewa Falls," *Chippewa Herald*, November 7, 1928.
183. Kenneth Whyte, *Hoover: An Extraordinary Life in Extraordinary Times* (New York: Knopf, 2017).
184. "Lafollette Is an Easy Victor," *Chippewa Herald*, November 7, 1928.
185. Minutes, Women of the Ku Klux Klan in Chippewa Falls, No.31.
186. "Ada Gillette Is Called by Death," *Chippewa Herald*, November 5, 1928.
187. "Ada Gillette Funeral Held Here Yesterday," *Chippewa Herald*, November 8, 1928.
188. "Ford Hub Cap Only Clue in Fatal Crash: Lorston Lynn, 13, Killed by Hit-Run Driver," *Chippewa Herald*, November 12, 1928.
189. "Obituary of J.E. Ellsworth," *Chippewa Herald*, November 12, 1928.
190. Minutes, Women of the Ku Klux Klan in Chippewa Falls, no. 32.

Chapter 3

191. *Kloran or Ritual*, Women of the Ku Klux Klan.
192. *Monthly and Quarterly Kligrapp Reports, 1927–1931*, Women of the Ku Klux Klan, University of Wisconsin Digital Collections.
193. United States Census Bureau, 1930 United States Federal Census.

194. "Heard About Town—Lekvin Birth," *Chippewa Herald*, September 18, 1928.
195. Minutes, Women of the Ku Klux Klan in Chippewa Falls, no. 33.
196. "The Weather on January 16, 1929," Midwestern Regional Climate Center, https://mrcc.illinois.edu.
197. "Hard Times Dance Party," Brown Paper Tickets, www.brownpapertickets.com.
198. Minutes, Women of the Ku Klux Klan in Chippewa Falls, no. 34.
199. *Constitution and Laws of the Women of the Ku Klux Klan*.
200. Ibid.
201. Minutes, Women of the Ku Klux Klan in Chippewa Falls, no. 35.
202. "Frank B. Chase Dies Suddenly at Home Here," *Chippewa Herald*, February 13, 1929.
203. "Chase Funeral Held," *Chippewa Herald*, February 16, 1929.
204. Minutes, Women of the Ku Klux Klan in Chippewa Falls, no. 36.
205. "Fear February Death Rate May Exceed that of January," *Chippewa Herald*, March 11, 1929.
206. "L. Butterfield Called by Death," *Chippewa Herald*, March 11, 1929.
207. U.S. Const. amend XVIII.
208. "State, City Officials Speak in Opposition to Referendum; Dixon Cites Crowded Dockets," *Eau Claire Leader*, March 31, 1929.
209. "Joint Resolution for Referendum on State Prohibition," Wisconsin Session Laws 1929, https://docs.legis.wisconsin.gov.
210. "Duncan on Referendum," *Eau Claire Leader*, April 4, 1929.
211. "State, City Officials Speak," *Eau Claire Leader*.
212. Minutes, Women of the Ku Klux Klan in Chippewa Falls, no. 37.
213. "State Votes Wet by Huge Majority: Repeal of Dry Law Favored by 125,000 Margin," *Eau Claire Leader*, April 4, 1929.
214. Ken Moraff, *It Happened in Wisconsin* (Las Vegas, NV: Amazon Publishing, 2013).
215. United States Census Bureau, 1930 United States Federal Census.
216. "W.R.C. Holds Election of Officers for Year," *Chippewa Herald*, December 10, 1929.
217. Minutes, Women of the Ku Klux Klan in Chippewa Falls, no. 38.
218. Keeping Membership Active, bulletin issued by the Wisconsin Realm of the Ku Klux Klan, November 1924.
219. Chippewa County Deed, Volume 42, #1829030, March 1, 1929, Warranty Deed for Parcel, Chippewa County Courthouse, Chippewa Falls, WI.
220. "For Sale. Midway Garage," *Chippewa Herald*, February 8, 1927.

221. "Nihart-Sippel," *Eau Claire Leader*, October 8, 1920.
222. "Chippewa Society," *Eau Claire Leader*, November 27, 1928.
223. "Hallie Farmer Dies Suddenly," *Chippewa Herald*, August 29, 1927.
224. Minutes, Women of the Ku Klux Klan in Chippewa Falls, no. 39.
225. WKKK Imperial Letter to All Klanswomen, May 28, 1929, University of Wisconsin Digital Collections.
226. Ibid., June 3, 1929.
227. Minutes, Women of the Ku Klux Klan in Chippewa Falls, no. 40.
228. Ibid., no. 41.
229. Ibid., no. 42.
230. "Mrs. Anna Rude Called by Death," *Chippewa Herald*, July 10, 1929.
231. WKKK Imperial Klaliff Letter to Tess Trainer, July 17, 1929, University of Wisconsin Digital Collections.
232. Minutes, Women of the Ku Klux Klan in Chippewa Falls, no. 43.
233. Ibid., no. 44.
234. United States Census Bureau, 1930 United States Federal Census.
235. "Mrs. Nettie Bollom," *Eau Claire Leader*, August 30, 1972.
236. "O.A. Bollom Is Taken by Death," *Chippewa Herald*, August 10, 1959.
237. "One Hundred Fifty at W.C.T.U. Inter-County Meeting at Park Friday," *Chippewa Herald*, August 12, 1933.
238. Minutes, Women of the Ku Klux Klan in Chippewa Falls, no. 45.
239. Ibid., no. 46.
240. Ibid.
241. Letter Written by Tess Trainer, October 16, 1929, the University of Wisconsin Digital Collections.
242. "Enjoy Card and Bunco Party," *Chippewa Herald*, November 20, 1930.
243. "A Colorful Past, a Colorful End," *Eau Claire Leader*, September 26, 1993.
244. "Badger Club Will Give a Chicken Dinner," *Chippewa Herald*, August 4, 1930.
245. Minutes, Women of the Ku Klux Klan in Chippewa Falls, no. 47.
246. Letter from Edith M. Hunt, Fall 1929, University of Wisconsin Digital Collections.
247. Ibid.
248. "Stock Market Crash of 1929," History, A&E Television Networks, https://www.history.com.
249. Minutes, Women of the Ku Klux Klan in Chippewa Falls, no. 48.
250. "Fiery Cross Burned by Milwaukee Klan," *Eau Claire Leader*, November 13, 1929.
251. Minutes, Women of the Ku Klux Klan in Chippewa Falls, no. 49.

Chapter 4

252. Minutes, Women of the Ku Klux Klan in Chippewa Falls, no 50.
253. Ibid., no. 51.
254. Imperial Letter to Third Annual Klonverse of Province No. 2, Ellsworth Resolutions, 1930, University of Wisconsin Digital Collections.
255. Minutes, Women of the Ku Klux Klan in Chippewa Falls, "Attention!!! Patriot Americans—*The Fellowship Forum*."
256. "Dittmar Services," *Chippewa Herald*, January 22, 1951.
257. United States Census Bureau, 1930 United States Federal Census.
258. Minutes, Women of the Ku Klux Klan in Chippewa Falls, no. 52.
259. "Obituaries: Mrs. William Hansen," *Chippewa Herald*, March 10, 1964.
260. United States Census Bureau, 1930 United States Federal Census.
261. Ibid.
262. Minutes, Women of the Ku Klux Klan in Chippewa Falls, no. 53.
263. United States Census Bureau, 1930 United States Federal Census.
264. "Dairymen's Picnic at County Asylum Sunday Has Large Attendance," *Chippewa Herald*, September 8, 1931.
265. "Kill Second Plan to Slash Committees," *Chippewa Herald*, November 14, 1936.
266. "Victory School," *Chippewa Herald*, October 21, 1935.
267 "Chippewa High School News," *Chippewa Herald*, December 15, 1934.
268. Minutes, Women of the Ku Klux Klan in Chippewa Falls, no. 54.
269. Imperial Letter on Third Annual Klorero, Delavan Resolutions, 1930. University of Wisconsin Digital Collections.
270. Minutes, Women of the Ku Klux Klan in Chippewa Falls, no. 55.
271. Imperial Letter on Kligrapps and Klabees, June 21, 1930, University of Wisconsin Digital Collections.
272. Ibid.
273. Official Document—WKKK Realm of Wisconsin, August 25, 1930, University of Wisconsin Digital Collections.
274. "The Klan Disappears," *Eau Claire Leader*, November 23, 1930.
275. "Enjoy Card and Bunco Party," *Chippewa Herald*, November 25, 1930.
276. Minutes, Women of the Ku Klux Klan in Chippewa Falls, no. 56.

Chapter 5

277. Minutes, Women of the Ku Klux Klan in Chippewa Falls, no. 57.
278. Ibid., no. 58.

Afterword

1. D'Vera Cohn, "How US Immigration Laws and Rules Have Changed Through History," Pew Research Center, September 30, 2015, https://www.pewresearch.org.
2. Minwegen, "Reminiscences."
3. Lake Hallie, Wisconsin, local, interview by author, September 10, 2018.
4. "300 Patrons Present When Dry Agents Raid Roadhouse; Fourth Brewery Is Wrecked," *Eau Claire Leader-Telegram*, January 16, 1931.
5. "Up in Flames," *Eau Claire Leader-Telegram*, September 26, 1993.
6. *Death Certificate for Robbie Gill-Comer* (Los Angeles, CA: Registrar-Recorder/County Clerk, 1963).
7. *Death Certificate for Mary Gray Bishop* (Grand Rapids, Michigan Department of Health, 1946).
8. "Evangelist Malone to Lecture Tuesday," *Escanaba Daily Press*, September 10, 1939.
9. "The Rev. Pat Malone," *Star Tribune*, February 15, 1963.
10. "WCTU to Meet at Bollom Home," *Chippewa Herald*, August 3, 1934.
11. "Gospel Services," *Chippewa Herald*, February 23, 1935.
12. Anonymous interviews by author, June–August 2018.
13. "Letter to the Editor," *Chippewa Herald*, October 28, 1932.
14. Anonymous interview by author, Fifield, Wisconsin, August 18, 2018.
15. *Death Certificate for Tessie Leon Trainer* (Fifield: Wisconsin Board of Health, 1947).
16. Anonymous interviews by author, June–August 2018.
17. Ibid.

ABOUT THE AUTHOR

John E. Kinville is a local historian who teaches American government at Chippewa Falls Senior High School. He earned his bachelor of arts in broadfield social studies education at the University of Wisconsin–Eau Claire and his master of arts in history education at the University of Wisconsin–River Falls. Kinville is the founder of Flags4Fallen.org, an educational organization designed to honor his school's forty fallen American soldiers. He resides near Chippewa Falls, Wisconsin, with his wife, children and three cats.